T0086472

The
Irony
Of The Well

The Aftermath and Dark Side of Recovery from Mental Illness

OWEN STAPLES

THE IRONY OF THE WELL
THE AFTERMATH AND DARK SIDE OF
RECOVERY FROM MENTAL ILLNESS

iUniverse books may be ordered through booksellers or by contacting:

iUniverse
1663 Liberty Drive
Bloomington, IN 47403
www.iuniverse.com
844-349-9409

Because of the dynamic nature of the Internet, any web addresses or links contained in this book may have changed since publication and may no longer be valid. The views expressed in this work are solely those of the author and do not necessarily reflect the views of the publisher, and the publisher hereby disclaims any responsibility for them.

Any people depicted in stock imagery provided by Getty Images are models, and such images are being used for illustrative purposes only. Certain stock imagery © Getty Images.

ISBN: 978-1-6632-0856-9 (sc)
ISBN: 978-1-6632-0857-6 (e)

Library of Congress Control Number: 2020917361

Print information available on the last page.

iUniverse rev. date: 09/16/2020

"In order to be created, a work of art must first make use of the dark forces of the soul."
~Albert Camus

"The more you know, the less you need."
–Cody Lundin.

The more you know, the less you can accept about the toxic, disease of current society, the giant factory."
–Owen Staples

INTRODUCTION

A Modern-Day Awakening

The Irony of The Well...

To him, it is simple. One can either be part of the problem, the disease of living beyond what the earth can sustain, or part of the solution, well-being and the awakening. The awakened always asks himself/herself:

"Am I too inflexible insisting on being right side up when everyone and everything else is upside down?"

"Is it mad?

Am *I* mad?"

He finds himself at risk of losing his home. Nearly food insecure, and with hunger seeming more likely with each day he lacks income, he feels isolated and alone, hungry for human connection with like-minded people, commonality and even affection. He feels barely sane. He experiences real hunger with the accompanied guilt of having to use mortgage money to buy groceries. He feels like he must choose between the two. It is a slow, steady starvation he is experiencing, and it will only get worse.

His awakening experience holds true, the memory of it is indelible. He tests it and reflects on it many times and sure enough, it holds to the test of both modern science and ancient wisdom. He knows there is no denying what he experienced, that is, even if he *wanted* to deny it. He knows that he must share and attempt to tell everyone no matter what the consequences, about the sweet spring water, The Well, the right way, how it is not too late for humanity, and to help others find it. Not only must he invite them to The Well, but he must also convince them that it exists. For most, wells are make-believe at best, something of the past, kind of like fairies, a fantasy. A daunting task then? It is the understatement of the century.

By some, he is thought to be and is called lazy, irresponsible, stupid, crazy, childish, dreamy and just about every cuss word available, but he holds like a pit bull to what he knows to be true and real.

He knows the irony is that he is fully sane trying to live the correct life of an ideal human as he sees it; he tries to live the ideal, the better way in a world that is set up as, and continues on, collective irrationalism, with a willful disregard for the planet. He also knows that he is one of the only ones who sees it, and so most others who do not yet see, are innocent.

He never doubts; he never regrets. He just hangs on. Maybe his work, his talking, writing, praying, hoping, dreaming, trekking, longing will be heard and acted on by some, even if only a small handful of people, before he returns to the ground. Maybe it will awaken some before he dies and before the earth is damaged beyond repair—and maybe not. He just may be another "forgotten awakened one", whose words are not heeded until after they are long gone, which are, even then only heard by a few. He turns from this chilly thought with a shiver like the January winds, but he knows that it just may be the case.

Still, it is his hope with all humanity being so close to finally understanding that keeps him going; that is of course, combined with the very real threat of slow and steady calorie deficit, his permanent void, his lack of food, monetary cushion and even fellow human support. It is his knowledge of how close people are to a full awakening that gives him hope. It is the sight of how far we have come that tells him we can surely get it right now! It is also the sight of that last one hundred yards being the most challenging while we run out of time and squander resources that also rubs his nerves raw. It seems like his food insecurity is just the beginning of a permanent black-hole poverty, and his hunger could lead to actual starvation. Ah, the state of mind that accompanies food insecurity! He dreads starvation. He also welcomes it. It is at least a tangible reminder why he endures what he must to invite others to The Well that they do not know about—and don't believe exists. What manner of man would face such to tell the rest about it? Crazy? Maybe. Or, maybe the water really is that sweet, that blissful. The answer is simple: Any who are awake; any who have tasted of The Well will dedicate their life in telling others about it. Daily he tells himself: "I would rather be fully awake, fully alive than asleep, half dead and call it life; even worse, attempt to call it *living.*"

His memory of it is something like this: He arrives alone at The Well and The Spring. He soaks in The Spring and drinks from The Well. Not only are they beautiful beyond the imagination and senses, but "of another time and place" kind of beautiful. The water is the sweetest, most magical he has ever tasted. In fact, it is the only water—pure, and free of pollution. He relishes it, drinks it up and stays. He stays longer and longer and gives no thought to anything but that very moment, the sweet savor, the breath of heaven, the ancient, everlasting spring spoken of since the beginnings of human language and long before…. this is it! Then, like an apple falling from the tree upon one's head, his wake up comes *within* his awakening. He looks around him in this other dimension; he sees life-pure-things as they *can* be, and as life *is*– in its place and order.

But he also sees that he is totally alone as to his own kind; only a handful of people like him exist. The rest live anesthetized by media, politicians and healthcare ("disease-care") in an illusion and they do not see The Well. He knows they won't be able to fully understand what they cannot see, let alone give it a taste. He tries to show them in writing while jobless, on the verge of losing his home and his wife. This is when he is reminded of just how crazy he appears to others. No humans are there with him. Yet they are the ones who must taste of The Well and truly submerge in The Spring. The birds taste it daily. The trees taste it daily. The coyotes taste it daily. The insects, tigers, grass, snakes, spiders, dragonflies, whales, marsupials, pill bugs, trout, snakes and Kingfishers taste of it daily. They know of it. Humans do not. They once knew and they lost that knowledge. Throughout their collective journey they chose fear and denial instead of pure water.

Nature and wildlife are under no spell, no illusion, and so they live fully alive—fully growing in joy. Modern humanity does not. They need to be reminded; yet even when they are reminded, they may not choose the thing of which they were reminded. They are sometimes that stubborn, that prideful. The natural world cannot and will not destroy The Well, cannot destroy The Spring. Humans can destroy The Well, and humans will. He must risk everything to tell them, to warn them before it is too late for humanity and the earth.

Right after the peaceful bliss of his awakening, a sickening dread begins to brew throughout his innards. He is jerked out of heaven just long enough to know that he must return to hell on earth where he is so utterly alone, facing a second divorce, hungry and nearly homeless. He is given a few last moments with heaven and The Well as he attempts to wrestle with himself and with God. The irony of The Well is that it is selfish to stay there alone—even in the pure bliss that he has found. The irony, like the Elfin high life in Tolkien's brilliance, is that it is criminally selfish to remain there as long as deliberately placed misinformation about The Well and, yes, evil in its greedy, manipulative power and monopoly exist and still carry the day.

After his long day, his arduous journey, when he arrives at The Spring, and his torn, dirty, sweat drenched clothes come off, he has the blissfully relieving initial thought that they never again need adorn his body. He can live, never far from The Spring, and always quenched with the sweet well water, to forever soak in the pure spring, and forever, at last, to stay in heaven, "to go no more out"... –(New Testament, King James Version of the Bible) but immediately he realizes this is not so. Put them all back on he must. Come up out of The Spring, leave the heavenly well behind, he must. Continue to attempt to live on polluted water long enough to tell the rest of his fellows, he must. He has a battle with himself, a wrestle with God. He fights long and hard; and what seems like years as his heart is slowly suffocating beneath the dread of vast uncertainty which must be faced are only moments... he cannot stay alone, the very irony. He wants to stay; more than any desire he has ever experienced, he wants to stay. He tries every means of justification he can possibly find to stay...but the only option is to leave. He is angry at just how thoughtless, foolish, prideful and how selfish people can be! He is angry that humanity is in this situation. He also knows that it is not entirely their fault, that no one person is to blame, and that he was once just like them. He also knows of the sweetness of this well and how everlasting it is. He knows that it is criminally selfish to stay at The Well alone without accepting it as his life purpose to tell others about it. He knows just how sweet will be the water, when all (if any), decide to join him. He weeps. He cries long and hard. His tears are acidic with anger toward the stubborn blindness, the foolishness of his fellow humans and their ways and the greed of corporations and government that only see dollar signs and a chance to wield power. His tears are also about the sadness of leaving. He wishes he could slap each person on the planet in the face all at the same time so that he can stay, have them wake up and then drop them in The Spring, force them to taste of The Well to join him, where they will be healed, and where they will *see* and also want to stay. They will thank him ceaselessly; they will bow at his feet for insisting that they drink. He knows they will. But he also knows the importance of free will, and that force is not the answer. They must be invited and journey to The Well themselves to know it, to believe it, to see it, and to be sufficiently stripped and prepared for it; to experience the journey to The Well, where their thirst is finally quenched and their skin and entire being—cleansed.

He nearly decides to stay against all odds and in complete selfishness. A little selfishness never hurt anybody. After all, we're all a bit selfish. He does this more than once. He is nearly willing to face the criminal selfishness and is willing to accept that permanent title for the eternities. For a moment or two, he thinks he is winning the wrestle with God. But it is the permanent brand on his soul, the thought of unbounded joy that he knows is his if he gets up and tells others. This is enough. He knows that if he were to stay, The Well would become less sweet as it also would begin to vanish, and he wants to taste its sweetness forever. He also knows that people, the trees, the birds, the forests, the snakes and all animals would endure more suffering if he allows The Well to vanish. He knows that he can have this again if he truly does all that he can to invite everyone else also. It is this thought that causes him to stand up from The Spring, taste one last drink of truly pure water, the only pure water. He even takes a few more sips, five more, eight, ten in madness and a scorching rage at even his willingness to stand up! He takes even more water to wash the salty, acidic tears from his face, and the saline that found its way to his tongue. He tastes the salt, and with it he is slapped out of heaven. The rough landing makes him impatient and he is feeling ready. He hears the hope of the birds, fish, trees, snakes, and deer. He hears them, not with his ears, but he hears them all the same. He feels them all watching him, there is *hope for them through him.* He bids them farewell for now but knows without a doubt that he will return to stay. He may or may not be alone when he does; but it matters not. All that will matter at that time, is that he tried. The Well is the only source of life. All creatures except people have chosen it. To choose it is to live…. whether alone, or with all, he will return to stay. He will live. This, the creatures accept. The sight, their beauty feeds him in joy where he grows. It affords him the strength to continue what he must finish, the means to an end. He knows this is true.

CHAPTER 1

"What Happened, Man?"
(2010-2011)

It is 2011. He is married. He has a job. He has a house next to a beautiful forest and nature trail in which he finds solace and wisdom. He and his wife have a family of rescued companion animals for which they both provide and care. He has been through the hell of, and recovery from, mental illness.

Despite all of this, he realizes and finally accepts that he cannot live a lie. He has been to the ocean floor—hell and back, and he cannot pretend that the puddle in the parking lot caused by the sprinkler being left accidentally running is okay, and further that the puddle constitutes the world. He knows there is more, that there is an ocean of knowledge to explore. He would be letting down not only himself, but also the animals, trees and his fellow humans if he were to settle and pretend that he doesn't know. Most of all, he knows he will not find peace unless he at least tries to tell and helps others to see and taste The Well.

What is a guy to do? He's trying to hold on to everything he has while carefully orchestrating and managing the patchwork of life—work, marriage, and caring for the pets that he and his wife have adopted. It's a delicate balancing act where "trapeze artist" is added to his repertoire of skills. Still, losing just one of these patches of his life could mean losing everything.

He has learned that those of us in American society live smack in the middle of the Cross and the Crown. The current American dream (we'll call it the dream of most Americans), is based on distorted half-truths and implications that there are guarantees in life. The current trap, the attempt to live the American dream, does not make one stronger; it makes one weaker, and it benefits the richest few while the rest have to scramble to figure out a way to make ends meet. It zaps dreams and happiness. It might work best for you if you are married, straight, white, Christian, and male. Even then, if you are lucky you only find yourself in the shrinking middle class. This is current reality. Yet it is the lie, the illusion, based on a worn out and shaky foundation insisting that it must be this way as the current model of capitalism. The current model uses a person-blame approach, instead of a system-blame approach where more responsibility or emphasis is placed on the system. A complete overhaul of the existing model is needed. The "perfection" that can be purchased at Wal-Mart is built on a lie, on denial. America has become an oligarchy designed to benefit the few at the expense of the many.

He didn't see through the system as he does now, so his battle with meds, mental illness and misplaced priorities took his life on a fifteen-year detour. During that 15-year hardship, he learns quickly that he is a meager slave. He was brought up and conditioned to believe that doing what people do, the endless cycle of borrowing, paying, earning, and spending, affords them power and happiness. But going deeply into debt to be a hero and take care of one's wife and kids, going to school to get a higher paying job to pay for your shelter for the next thirty years, does not give one power and strength. He learns many things and is empowered to realize that having his house, his job and even his love relationship are the illusion. With the way things are set up in society he has very little real power; his power ends as far as he can throw a rock, and lasts only as long as he is willing to remain a slave. He bought into the illusion that he had his house, his finances, his wife and their family of companion animals all under control—living the dream. But he paid the price. In the end, these belonged to the puppet master. They were not his—not his house, not his job. Even his wife, his beloved queen could only be called his for as long as he could bring home a certain standard of income. Should he fail at this, she will go away and be "repossessed" like everything else.

After finding The Well-Spring and realizing how things are supposed to be and just how backwards and upside down they are from that ideal, he becomes spent and weak from trying to have and keep, trying to hold on to the heavenly well-spring, the source of true strength, well-being, true life, peace and happiness. The forest next to where he lives offers him a peace, solace, and retreat that is irreplaceable. Looking at history, he sees that humanity has indeed come so far; he is baffled that they stumble on the final course.

Rewind Time…2004-2010

Just before his awakening and vision of a better way, there he was in 2010 working at a hardware store, daily trading in his authentic self and his dreams in attempt to earn a buck, or ten of them per hour to be exact. In doing this, he learned that he is outside himself, beside himself, someone other than himself, near his wits end, living a lie to earn his meager $10 per hour to make ends meet and pay for his home, utilities and food. It is exhausting. Since he reaches the point of being beside himself, outside himself, he writes in third person about the largely immature boy that he was at the time of this 15-year hardship, since hindsight is better than foresight.

The structure of an irrational system supports a sick society; the structure is flawed because it is based on lies, on deliberately and conveniently misplaced truths and guarantees that should not be called such because they cannot be guaranteed. They are promises that cannot be kept. The earth is fat with abundance, but few people realize it because resources are all caught up by the monopoly.

"There is enough for everyone's need but not everyone's greed." -Mahatma Gandhi.

Because Jobs Are the One Thing That Can't Be Purchased From the Shelf at Wal-Mart

In 2004 he got a job at a hardware store. As mentioned in The Wellness Diaries the job was a miracle to obtain, let alone *retain* it. Considering his diagnosis at the time and his prescription medications, the outcome looked grim. One psychiatrist told him it was unlikely that he could even get a job. But get one he did, and in fact he was employed there for seven years. The job helped him to grow in confidence and skills. Still, near the end of his time there, he realized that he could do better and that he wanted something else. He could not see that job as his lifelong career.

He was grateful beyond words to this hardware store for hiring him—essentially a leap of faith to hire someone taking prescription medications for a diagnosed mental illness. However as he gained seniority, his work conditions morphed to where he was scheduled to work a swing shift ending at 11 pm followed by opening the store the very next morning at 6 am. This was indeed a difficult schedule and it began to seem like he was owned by his employer. He began to feel trapped and that he was basically a slave.

One of the most frustrating aspects of the job was how it interfered and sabotaged his relationship. For several months in a row he was scheduled to close the store; but because his queen left early in the morning, and he in the afternoon, they rarely saw each other. Through the weeks that passed, he expressed to his queen his increasing frustration and job dissatisfaction. She offered words of encouragement and told him of her own experiences working retail and how relieved she felt when she resigned from those jobs.

Those seven years at the hardware store helped him to get a start in life. It gave him valuable experience, a huge boost of confidence that he so desperately needed at that time as explained in The Wellness Diaries. Working in the nursery department helped stir a remembrance of his interest in plants and the natural world, and from his employment there, he learned how beneficial the natural world is to his well-being. He is very grateful to have learned this. He is also grateful for all the customer compliments he received regarding his excellent service. He appreciates his supervisors talking up his ability and skill level with customers and for using him as a successful example to other employees during team meetings.

The time spent at the hardware store was seven years well-spent and he regrets none of it. He is grateful beyond measure to all supervisors and coworkers who spent the time with him, as well as to organizations involved in helping him to acquire and retain the job. He had friends at the hardware store. They were the next closest thing to family in his life. At eight hours a day, five days a week, he spent more time with these people than with his own wife and social circles! He became close to some of his coworkers and even to some of the customers. He enjoyed the good talks and working beside them.

He is automatically faced with two perspectives. He is on one hand grateful, and on the other discontented. This pinprick conundrum was what helps him to realize that he has outgrown the hardware store and the fifty square mile world in which he and his queen then lived. He realizes that there is more to life than working 9-5 until 65 and that he wants something else, and that staying in his current position would be settling for mediocrity, feeling unsatisfied, and always aware that there is more.

It was after he adopted a vegan diet in 2009 that he began to read and study extensively on the topics that interested him, including history, plants, spirituality, the law of attraction, animal rights, health and nutrition. He discovered just how much is out there! He read many inspiring books and articles. It was at this time he realized that he also had a dream. He looks at his life, and his new change of being vegan and enjoying good health once again. He wonders just how feasible it all is for the long term. He realizes that the swing shift is not good for his mental and physical health or his levels of stress. He knows that he will not be content to stay there at the hardware store for the rest of his life as he had planned when being hired in 2004, at which point he was ecstatic about just being able to hold down a full-time job. He has grown since then.

At the hardware store, in order to be eligible for full-time status and all the benefits that come with it such as paid vacation and health benefits, employees are required to have what is called "open availability." That is, to work anytime within the store hours of 6 am to 10 pm. Typically this meant working either the 6 am-3 pm shift, or the 2 pm-11 pm shift.

The haphazard schedule was causing him stress; his body could not adjust to any type of rhythm or routine, the very thing it needed. He didn't want to do it anymore. Maybe it was mere boredom with the schedule; or, perhaps his instincts led him correctly and the odd schedule really was beginning to wear down his health and peace of mind. His concern for his well-being increased his dissatisfaction, contributed to his stress and, he sensed it was putting him in danger of a mental health relapse.

At that time and having worked at the hardware store for six years he finally decided in 2010 to ask his psychiatrist who prescribed his medications for a doctor's note so that he could continue to work but also have a consistent schedule. The psychiatrist provided him with the note, preventing him from being scheduled to work past 6 pm for the time being. The doctor's note worked well for several months, but to the dismay and unrest of his coworkers; they were becoming increasingly resentful at his fixed schedule, doctor's note or not, which is not in line with the company's policy. Every other full-time employee was required to keep open availability for full-time employees. Why should he be different? On one hand, he understood the rules and that business is business. It is hard to bend them, especially within the rules, regulations, policies and procedures of a large corporation. On the other hand, though, it was detrimental to his mental health. His ability to think, feel and reason clearly were being impaired. *Couldn't this be the exception?* this was his livelihood. Everything (what little he had) including his mortgage, pets and his queen was built upon this meager wage. He felt so incredibly stuck, so trapped. The swing shift was truly dragging him onto the depths of despair; it put him into a state of debilitation (as explained in the first memoir, <u>The Wellness Diaries</u>.) If only his coworkers could understand that his entire being was being virtually threatened by the swing shift.

There is only forward, and no going backwards.

So there he was, just recently having purchased his first home, a small 1110 square foot condo in Sherwood Park, when, as explained in <u>The Wellness Diaries</u>, his wife's car was totaled in a series of strange events that set them back. They shared the one car, having sold his truck to cut expenses.

Gone were the days of waking up in the morning and driving ten minutes on the freeway to get to work. With only one vehicle which they shared, he had to take the bus to the hardware store, which, after a long westward detour, was an hour each way. He would leave the house at five in the morning. Sometimes he would ride his bicycle, (also one full hour) to get to work. To complicate matters further, he still had reptiles, which he kept at his at his former residence (parents' house), since there was not enough room at his condo. He had to stop on the way home to feed and care for them.

Packing his vegan meals was also time-consuming. His coworkers got to "analyze" his meals as he sat down to eat lunch each day. At first this was fine, but in short time, snide comments began along with tension and misunderstanding. He learned that he preferred to go outside to eat his lunch, but this increased the negative comments about "hippie" and "tree hugger." At first, the comments weren't so bad, and he enjoyed excitedly sharing information about his new vegan diet and healthy lifestyle that benefits both the earth and people, and about the way things are supposed to be. But eventually, the comments started to drag him down. Many questions were not born of genuine interest; they were for their own amusement and with intent to mock, uncover contradiction, to use it against him later and for gossip appeal. He now admits that at the time he strutted around with his share of arrogance also, which fanned the flames—so many of his foolish mistakes of the past can be chalked up to his being emotionally immature at that time. Hindsight is better than foresight; still, enough was enough. While some of his coworkers were supportive, over time, some became quite rude regarding his diet, his doctor's note, the schedule, and virtually who he was. He was the target of gossip, backbiting and slander that was fueled by already existing envy and bitterness about his fixed schedule. It is true, he realized, that it really wasn't fair to his coworkers to continue in his fixed schedule with doctor's note in a company where open availability is the rule…

You are probably asking the same question that he eventually had to ask: "Who does this?! Who insists on continuing this way? Well, either someone with a touch of insanity, or tenacity beyond this world. Maybe he had a touch of both.

Around this time, he learned some key information through his B.R.I.D.G.E.S (Building Individuals Dreams and Goals Through Education and Support) class by the Utah chapter of the National Alliance for Mental Illness (N.A.M.I.). The thalamus, a very primitive part of the brain responsible for sleep is typically smaller in people with schizophrenia. Whether or not this was the case for him, he inferred that he must compensate by proactively striving to set himself up for sound sleep. He must make his sleep world larger—quiet with a dark, cool room.

With the doctor's note requesting that he be allowed to work only between the hours of nine A.M. and six P.M. and the underlying tension and bitterness it caused, something had to give. However, the only place to put him with his new limited hours of availability is on the dreaded 'front end' as a cashier. The front end was known for its problems of moody and frequently sick cashiers. There was much tension; one could call it drama. He was also assigned to help in the hardware department, essentially bouncing back and forth between the two as a cashier and a customer service associate in the hardware department. Due to company policies, rules, procedures, regulations it was not an option for him to stay outside in the busy garden department where he grew, learned and developed his knowledge, skill and talent, finely tuned to an impressive resume' and a file filled with customer compliments, engaged in the work that he enjoyed to the maximum. After all, this was what he had grown to love and where he preferred to be. Instead, he was to be bounced back and forth. It was becoming increasingly problematic trying to find a place to put him within the confines of his doctor's note and fixed schedule. Instead of being outside in bright, warm sunshine, surrounded by plants, insects and birds, as he had been for the past several years, he was often required to come inside to a dark warehouse as a cashier… He felt the letdown. As the department manager of the hardware department once said in a bout of frustration with everything but especially with his lack of knowledge in hardware, "I don't get it; take a person out of garden who knows everything there is to know about plants, and stick him in hardware…"

One cold, gray day in January 2011, he decided that he was done. He could not take it any longer. He was going to leave the hardware department and quit his job, the only long-term position he'd had his entire life. He was so confident in his decision that he took the lock off his locker and cleaned it out. He told no one of his plans to not return to work. He did not give two weeks' notice.

At the end of his shift, he got in the car with his queen who had driven the fifteen minutes through back road traffic to pick him up from work. He was unprepared to tell her also of his desperate situation, all too aware of the current financial bind that she was in too. He had been feeling so incredibly stuck. This made him sad and depressed. The outlook seemed hopeless, like all his energy was spent working, preparing food for, or getting to work. He seemed to live in a straitjacket. In fact, he was well on his way to needing more meds, regressing back to square one after all his progress with managing his mental health on minimal medications. All the discovery, exploration, newly acquired knowledge and health from his vegan diet and lifestyle change was about to be all for naught. Yet the thought of just continuing as things were felt like a prison sentence.

That evening, he called one of his confidants, his sister, and shared with her his plan to not return. Through a long phone conversation, she convinced him that he must return to work. He knew that she was right about several things, but one main thing was the fifty-pound barbell to the load that is already strained: The hardware store was his first real job, being the longest held job on his record. Seven years in one place of employment shows impressive merit and dedication on a resume' or job application. To essentially walk out of his place of employment, the only form of real work experience in his professional life after seven years without giving two weeks' notice, and with a known history of mental illness really seemed at the time like career suicide. But staying there as things were, would lead to real suicide. He was convinced to bring his padlock back to work the next day. (It was a good thing he didn't tell anyone).

The long phone conversation ended with him convinced but feeling completely/utterly deflated with that all too familiar, heavy tar feeling once again, "This is life?! To finally arrive home in the evening, eat dinner, have a few hours with his queen to then wake up and do it all again? Life is supposed to be enjoyed, not dreaded!" As a being, fully alive, one is supposed to be able to breathe. But he felt like he was slowly but surely suffocating. He felt so utterly trapped.

He knew that for his queen and their animal children he must somehow continue, taking one day at a time. He dearly loved his queen, their shared cats, small dog and reptiles, the story of how they met, the combining of two families, the life they had built. He wanted to do everything he could for these. How though, when he himself could barely breathe? When every day was spent trying to figure out a way to continue, to continue to merely survive? He knew that he must try something else. After all, he would be no good at all for supporting and pulling his share for those that he loves if he is living a lie and is utterly depressed. He knew he must do something—something. He began to apply to a few other jobs in the area. He wasn't exactly sure how yet, but he knew he must make a change. Certainly, there will be other jobs...

He reached the point in the summer of 2011 that was "now or never." He was very aware of the increasing tension and resentment among his coworkers caused by his doctor's note, his set schedule, and even his vegan diet. He suspected that they are looking for a reason to let him go. He felt so stuck. The dilemma was if he left, there was no other job lined up to replace it (even though he had applied at several), but if he stayed and got fired, there would be even fewer employment options. He knew that it was time to act. He was dealing with a year's buildup of tension, disgruntled coworkers, their comments, their tense silence, and resentful expressions. He reminded himself that it was the job he could get at that time and that it had served its purpose and was not destined to become his life career. He had read so many inspiring books, watched inspirational talks. He knew that he had to face the unknown and take the leap. He knew that he preferred this, even death, to living a lie, pretending that he still loved his schedule and that he was okay with settling for living in a trap. He knew that he must take the risk and jump off the cliff, hoping that where he jumped, the river was deep enough to cushion his landing.

The current pace and model of American society is outdated. It has been the same collective momentum and pace since the industrial revolution and a change is long overdue

"Think I need a devil to help me get things right
Hook me up a new revolution cause this one is a lie. We
sat around laughing and watched the last one die…
We'll live happily ever trapped if you just save my life
Run and tell the angels that everything's alright…"
– Foo Fighters, "Learn to Fly"

He decides to do so. His 311 songs are with him giving him courage and much needed positive vibes. He wakes up on that bright June morning and knows that he will find the strength to do it that day. It is inevitable, and it must be done. He doesn't know how he will muster up the courage, but he knows he must and that he will. Many things happen that day which confirm his decision and motivate him. He walks in the store for his shift and greets two cashiers who not only ignore him, but one female even shoulder bumps him as she passes.

During the planting season, he could be around the environment that he loved since, fortunately he was allowed to at least be a cashier in the garden center during their busy season. While cashiering outside did not allow his interacting with plants and with the customers about the plants that he had grown to enjoy so much and at which he excelled, he at least was in the garden center, the environment in which he was most comfortable and familiar.

But it is June and the planting season is winding down quickly and the garden center will soon close for the season. Rick, a supervisor that he likes comes out to inform him of the latest updates from the front end. This is his chance. All supervisors are intimidating but he likes Rick. Rick was manageable. He is all too aware of the promise that he made himself as his supervisor is updating him. As the anxiety builds for what he must do, he cannot focus or listen. The supervisor finishes his update. This is his chance! Waiting as Rick makes his closing statements, Owen is polite and shows that he is listening, and he does so with nods, and "okay". The pause after Rick's update was his chance.

He doesn't take it. He chickens out! He just can't do it. Rick begins to walk away to the front end. He watches as his supervisor exits the garden center, his confidence wanes with waxing frustration. His uncertainty continues. He feels like he knows nothing and that he barely exists. He promised himself. He must fulfill that promise! He doesn't know how. His anxiety continues to build. There he is pacing at the register like a caged tiger. During those next few moments, he was on the verge of either blowing up or breaking down. He is not allowed to be more than ten feet from his station at the cash register, so he could not go to Rick for a second shot. He is already anxiously kicking himself for not fulfilling his promise to himself. He doesn't know how, when, or whether he will do it at this point. He begins to doubt that he has it in him. This thought makes him depressed and very anxious.

At his most painful moment—limbo coupled with gray uncertainty—he notices Rick walking toward him again. Can it be? He must be dreaming! His heart leaps from the anxiety of the previous moment, turning to a rush of hope that he may not have missed his chance after all. After all, why was he so afraid? It is only his livelihood, but it is his only livelihood. This thought leaves him practically paralyzed with fear. He practically rebukes himself cracking the whip on his own back. "This is your chance. Do it this time!"

Rick walks up to him and makes a joke about the style of hat displayed on an end cap, how one can't tell if it is for fishermen or gardeners. In his preoccupation and nervousness, he doesn't really get the joke, so he gives an awkward courtesy laugh and is silent, again paralyzed with fear. Maybe he just can't do it. Maybe he won't. Rick begins to walk away again; he delivered the joke and Owen didn't receive it, so it's time to return to the front end.

Just do something, anything! So, he does. It all just comes out. He jumps off the cliff. Knowing nothing about what his next step will be, he just does it, jumps, hoping for everything to fall into place.

"Hey Rick, um I have something to tell you."

"Sure bud, whatcha got?"

"I'm going to turn in my two weeks... I'm not doing this anymore, I'm done." It came out a bit harder than he had planned, but great anxiety will do that.

Rick's gray moustache made him appear firm, militant and intimidating. Rick pursed his lips in concern and empathy. He was also surprised but stayed professional. "Oh... okay... So, what's your plan? Are you going somewhere else, or...?"

"No, I don't have another job lined up yet, been applying though. I just want to do my own thing, some more writing or maybe something more directly involving plants. I've been here for seven years now and I want to branch out a bit."

Rick's stare was full of curiosity; his mind gauging and his clear eyes were like the hands of a clock, but he stopped it all in a business-like fashion. "Okay...Alright, I'll let the front end know."

As Rick walks away, the anxiety ratchets down on his nerves. He had done it, but the 'what-if' thoughts begin to plague his mind. Initially, he feels anxious and self-critical about his delivery. He realizes that his approach made it appear that his frustration was with Rick and his joke about the garden hat.

He had much respect for Rick. Rick had a temper and was always a straight shooter, but had a personal touch as well, and tried to lighten up the grinding routine of retail from time to time, using goofy hats, for example as much needed distractions. He is concerned about Rick. He understands that his own communication is not the most effective. He hopes the guy didn't take it personally and realizes in the end that it was not him.

After all, America is all business. Business is business. If only he'd known then what he knows now. If only American businesses put as much merit, respect and concern for fellow coworkers that he did as he gave the news to Rick. But business is business, so sweat it he should not. But sweat it he does.

He did it! That was the good news, but for the next hour, anxiety ants begin to crawl on his body as he stands there alone with his cash register in the garden center; he is on the verge of a panic attack. He spends the next hour of what feels like a painful free-fall off the cliff from which he'd just jumped. The free-fall is supposed to be the easiest part, not the hardest, and it is not supposed to take so long to reach the river where he could then swim to new ground!

One of his trusted associates, a long time plant vendor, notices his anxiety and asks if he is okay. He confides in her and she provides just the right words of encouragement saying that she knows of nobody else as knowledgeable about plants as he is and that he will surely find something elsewhere. He begins to feel better.

His return of confidence came not a moment too soon because minutes after his conversation with Rick, during his bi-polar battle with the anxiety ants, alone at the cash register with his "what if" thoughts and his panicked plan-making, the manager from the front end pays him a visit to the garden center, presumably to determine the sincerity of his intentions.

Did he really do that? The front end was apparently as surprised as he was.

"Rick tells me you're turning in your two weeks; what's going on?"

Shyly and still intimidated by his anxiety-ridden free-fall and now faced by another intimidating supervisor, he reluctantly explains with initial fumbling speech. He is surprised by the bravery that he is already finding on the way down from his free-fall. He explains that he disagrees with pushing credit onto people and encouraging so much debt; it is against his principles, and that he wants to branch out.

As a supervisor of a giant corporation that is taught and teaches employees daily to encourage the use of new credit cards to customers, she was stunned, but respectfully accepts his formal two weeks' notice. It is the point of no return...

He knows that the real challenge is to get his queen to jump with him, to accept and not panic at the choice he made, even though they had talked about it beforehand. When he does tell her, her worried face increases his pressure. She is also afraid, and is trying not to panic, which increases his own fear, but since they had already discussed it some, she gives him her support. He appreciates this.

CHAPTER 2

To Understand the Beginning is to Understand the Middle and the Ending
(1988-2003)

It is essential to rewind yet again...

He grew up in Utah, a typically large Mormon family. He was the youngest, a surprise, the last of seven siblings. He was much younger than his older siblings, his sister closest to him in age being eight years older than he. Later in life he learned that he was an accident child. This was hard news to take. "Mr. Live On Purpose" was not even born on purpose, his mom having given birth to him in her forties.

But he still had plenty of fun in his youth. In fact, he was an uncle by the time he was nearly two years old. He grew up with nieces and nephews close to his age that he saw and interacted with often. They were more like friends than family. Their friends mixed well with his friends from school and it was great times. It could be said of his childhood that growing up was like being the oldest, youngest and the only child all at the same time, merely a matter of time and place until the role switched, and switch often it did.

Growing up was a great deal of fun. Throughout grade school, junior high and into high school, he had a big group of friends. His siblings will say that he grew up spoiled. Despite the protests of his mom, his dad virtually got him anything and everything he wanted, except for a pet snake. His dad was terrified of snakes and wouldn't allow one in the house. A pet snake would have to wait for later years when he grew up and had his own house.

Still, there were plenty of adventures to be had. Growing up he had fancy toys, bikes, scooters, He-Man toys, and the inevitability of Nintendo games popular in the late 1980's. There was always the traditional group of friends that he ran with in fun adventures, innocent mischief and continuous frolic. As a young boy he was fascinated by animals, read books about them all throughout grade school, and kept several pets. The fish, lizards, alligators, wolves, snakes, badgers, coyotes, lions, many creatures of the earth caught and held his attention, and he had his favorites. These faded slightly and briefly during the teen years when his interests shifted more toward girls and friends.

The Runt of the Litter

Family life was different for him being so much younger than the rest of his siblings with whom he shared the nest for only a short time as they moved on into their adult lives. By the time he was in seventh grade, he was alone with his parents in the household. At this time, his dad, who was raised on a farm and was also a farmer for the first part of his life was very sick with type-2 diabetes and had recently lost a contract with a successful landscaping maintenance company. It had been the business which paid the bills and allotted the life of affluence to which the Staples family had become accustomed. His mom had to return to school to earn her master's degree so she could work as a speech therapist, make ends meet, pay the bills and mortgage, provide for a young teen's sick dad, and a young and growing teenage boy. It was critically necessary for her to obtain a job with insurance to cover the many doctor visits, insulin injections and prescription medications.

It can often be said about the youngest in a family that they dance to the beat of a different drum than do the other siblings. By the time the youngest is born, parents are generally worn out from raising the other kids. On one hand it is said by older siblings about the youngest that they "get away" with much more; that by this later phase in the family game, parents are less strict and have learned through trial and error and experience about parenting. (As if parents really know what they're doing anyway, since they learn as they go also.) On the other hand, from the perspective of the youngest, the runts sometimes experience feelings of low self-esteem and self-worth, often feeling left out, excluded or left behind. It is ironic that the older siblings will often say about the youngest that he or she is spoiled, has much more, and gets away with much more than "we did."

The result is a cycle: the youngest searches out their own pursuits due to feeling left behind; then the youngest is blamed for not fitting in or not being up to speed with the other siblings. The youngest feels frustrated that their relationship to their parents is constantly compared to that of the other siblings, especially in adult life when they are expected to somehow suddenly "jump the gap" and behave in a foreign new role with their parents.

The relationship of older siblings to parents is totally different that the relationship of the last-born to parents. It is like comparing the 1940's to the 1990's; there is no comparison. The other siblings naturally become caught up in the busy-ness of their own lives and are afforded a natural transition through life from being the child, to adolescent, until they triumphantly fledge the nest with support and approval from Mom and Dad. These transitions of each sibling adds multiple layers to the dynamic, so by the time the youngest is in early formative stages, the family dynamic is a confusing whirl of mixed needs and agendas.

The youngest, then, moves on to find their own identity, musings, and hobbies, separate and distinct from his siblings lest their whole identity get swallowed up. The youngest must compensate for and attempt to make sense of the frenzy while distinguishing their own individuality. Later, they may learn to more fully explore and cultivate the found musings and hobbies. With the unspoken order and many unwritten rules come potential problems from the assumptions and expectations caused by that order.

Such was the case in the author's life. His older siblings say he was spoiled rotten, having everything he ever wanted (except that damn snake that he wasn't allowed to have until 2002). But if this was the case, why from 2001-2006 did he feel the need to fill his parents' basement with multiple pet reptiles as written in The Wellness Diaries? Why was he forever searching for something, forever clawing? The answer is that these are a screaming, an outward expression of something he knows he is lacking, unsure of what it is or how to discover it. It was an attempt to fill a void. That was indeed the hardest part—that he didn't even know what was driving his frenzied acquisition of animals—being so lacking something— starved and attempting to fill a void with exterior things instead of seeking to fill it from within. In 2005 he even took out a loan for a $5,000 lizard mansion. This was one of his financial mistakes as a newly wedded man in his first marriage as discussed in The Wellness Diaries. But how was he to know at the time? He was still emotionally a boy.

People don't realize how starved they are until they partake of real nourishment, the thing that they *need* and are lacking.

It is the author's opinion that the youngest are affected by a different cluster of mental health issues. There is no wonder then that the youngest can suffer from what he has observed and calls "love absorption disorders." These can occur even in the most loving of homes because often the youngest can process, act upon and 'absorb' love differently.

The diagnosis of schizophrenia actually should have been the least of his concerns, because his newfound state of health as described in <u>The Wellness Diaries</u> uncovers his deeper issues of abandonment, feelings of lacking love, social isolation and tendency toward cruelty. He learned rather early that it would benefit him greatly to develop his compassionate side, and to turn toward love, light and life.

The youngest of the family is born on a minivan full of people that is cruising down the freeway at 75 MPH. Just short of instantly out of the womb, they are expected to keep pace with everyone and everything. It should come as no surprise that later in life the youngest are known as little spitfires, seeming to others that they have something to prove and are full of spunk; neither should it come as a surprise that they prefer their own pace, style and ways of doing things. They could easily be given their own acronym, Y.W.A. (youngest with attitude). It is unfortunate that this different style taken on by the youngest of doing, learning and growing is often misunderstood.

Niceness or passivity is often mistaken for being of a "lesser intelligence." The youngest is sometimes perceived by others as "slow" or, to the other extreme, as abrasive. They may become bullies; they may be called names in childhood. They are misunderstood and, being different, they are often labeled or branded from an early age.

The youngest of the family often has abandonment issues, which can lead to the development of flawed viewpoints of being alone. They can easily feel isolated. They can be domineering and even nasty with others. To them, life often feels like they must either jump on the minivan that is going down the freeway at full speed or be left behind and that there is no in between. They have three seconds to make their decision. The youngest develops a different cluster of coping mechanisms and a vastly different lens of how they view the world.

In an ideal world there would be a self-expression playground for this bundled up energy and creativity, an encouraged outlet, a pace

that respects their style of learning. This is part of the problem—
in the current nature of society, to his knowledge, there is not.
Fortunately, there are always trade-offs and his younger days were
spent surrounded by many friends. The youngest often does have
many friends, even with their share of spunk they tend to develop
the types of personalities that are intriguing and attractive to others.
This helps them to make friends when young, to be reliable, and to
maintain these friendships throughout adulthood.

Having a sick and homebound dad was not without its benefits.
His dad was always there, at any time, day or night to talk with
him when he needed. This his dad did faithfully. They had some
very bonding talks. This is helpful for a young teen experiencing
the pressures of growing up in the world. He became very close to
his dear dad, so much that he learned to detest the word "father,"
feeling the term too heavy, formal, and confining to do justice to
the fantastic relationship he actually had with his dad.

In the fall of 1994, his junior year of high school, his dad's
diabetes turned fatal. He knew of no way, no person to continue the
caliber of conversation that he had relied on with his dad during his
crucial junior high school years. His dad's death didn't really sink in
for him until over a year later. In spite of the challenges, he managed
to graduate high school. During that time frame from grade school
through high school he was lucky to have many friends with his
parents' house as the main hangout. This helped him to ride out
and counterbalance his dad's untimely death.

The Missionary

Shortly after high school in the late nineties, he served a mission
for his church at that time, The Church of Jesus Christ of Latter
Day-Saints, aka LDS or Mormon. He spent two years in Eastern
Canada. During this relatively short period, he learns a lot about life
and the general "cathedral of Christendom."

Rules and lifestyles for missionaries change occasionally to adapt to changes in modern life. He was among the last group of missionaries to still write handwritten letters each week to his family back in Utah. Being the early 1990's, email was still quite new at the time and it was strictly forbidden of missionaries. It was only the disobedient, 'apostate' missionary who set up his own email account to communicate with others.

He was one of only two, out of more than one hundred missionaries who ate a vegetarian diet in the Canada Halifax Mission. Continuing his vegetarian diet (and sometimes vegan, even if he knew little about the nutritional details at the time) for two years in Eastern Canada as a Mormon missionary was not without resistance from peers, fellow missionaries and colleagues, but it was part of the adventure and part of his training. Word spread quickly of the vegetarian elder. Many church members preferred to cook special meals for him; it was something different, challenging and less expensive than meat. One prospective church member (called "investigators" in mission lingo) had had no contact with missionaries for several years, and was possibly losing interest in the church. But when he met the vegetarian elder, his interest was renewed and he invited the missionaries over to taste his vegetarian lasagna. (It was without a doubt *excellent*.)

His experience as a missionary provided his first exposure to the many interrogative questions and he began learning to deflect, or counter argue this line of questioning. The questions were often not from an interested, receptive standpoint but instead from a place of insecurity and with the hope of catching contradictions and causing Elder Staples to chase his tail. The questions were often asked by fellow missionaries as well as church members, or during dinners at zone conference. (Zone conference is a gathering of mission participants from larger outlying areas.)

His dietary lifestyle was seen by some as intriguing and unique; for others it was extreme and weird. The Mormon doctrine of the "Word of Wisdom" clearly states to "eat meat sparingly" and states, "it is pleasing unto me that it (meat) should not be used," was often a topic of conversation and spirited debate. (The "Word of Wisdom" is section 89 of the larger Mormon scripture, The Doctrine and Covenants.)

He always sensed that there was something important about getting enough sleep, even in Canada. Even then, while so young and in his prime, sleep proved to be a challenge. He had not yet heard of sleep hygiene tips like keeping the room cool and as dark as possible, however he did learn of the general principle of going to bed and arising at about the same time each day. The regimented hours of mission life proved to work wonders for his mood, spiritual focus and well-being. In fact, within the first few weeks of his mission he learned just how incredibly beneficial it was for his well-being to have a regulated sleep routine.

He had also not yet learned of the importance of sleep in coping with stress, anxiety and/or symptoms of mental illness as written in The Wellness Diaries. As mentioned earlier about the smaller thalamus in people with schizophrenia, some people are successful in learning to manage quality sleep by finding ways of making their "sleep world" larger. This helps to compensate for the smaller thalamus, setting them up for the right amount of quality sleep and improving many aspects of health, especially memory and mental health.

The fourth area where he served his mission proved extra challenging in this way. He had been stationed in an apartment with three other elders (missionaries). Mission rules as per the "white handbook" say to arise each morning at 6:30 and retire at 10:30 pm. While he had not yet managed to do this without an alarm (a treasured ability he was to acquire in 2011), he arose faithfully by an alarm and retired by the times prescribed in the mission rules. It was very challenging that he was the only one interested in obeying this part of the mission rules. To the detriment of his mood and his important missionary work, his noisy companions made for poor, interrupted sleep.

How does only one out of four obey all the rules? He was supposed to get adequate sleep, retire and arise at the same time each day, not only to respect the rules, but also because it was crucial to his mental functioning. Unfortunately for him, the other three chose to disregard those rules.

He was desperate for quality sleep and longed to go off on his own to do so since that seemed to be what it would take. However, this was not allowed due to a rule to never be out of sight from one's "companion". (Each missionary is assigned a companion in the LDS faith) This "buddy system" also decrees that he must sleep in the same room with his companion, and the consequence for breaking that rule is harsher than for breaking the curfew rule. There was not enough space in an apartment with four elders to set up his own bedroom, nor was he allowed to do so. The rules forbade it all.

In apartments with four elders, there are to be two bedrooms and four beds. He became frustrated with the other elders and asked them nicely to stay quiet so he could sleep, but to no avail. He then tried drastic measures and confronted them with additional assertiveness. This didn't work either, and only served to annoy them. They found him a nag and too extreme, which caused tension. He was outnumbered by three of them. He felt it was his duty as a missionary to faithfully obey all the rules, while they found the rules pointless, and seemed to think that the rules didn't apply to them. They snapped back, and it all added up to thick tension in the apartment.

In this fourth and final area of his two-year mission, he had no alternatives. He was outnumbered, and for the final six months of his mission, his sleep patterns were disrupted. His mood, focus, and spiritual light suffer. During the first eighteen months of his mission, his excellent sleep rhythms had even helped him to avoid masturbation-a forbidden practice for Mormon missionaries. Yes, for the first 18 months of his two-year mission, he relied on nocturnal emissions only as tension release and they occurred weekly and sometimes twice weekly, for which he was teased by the others.

Still, he worked hard to not break this rule. The weekly nocturnal emissions were noticed by the other elders and it made for funny jokes, much laughter, and several comments: "stop thinking about girls," or, "you must have a problem." Even then he knew he was simply a healthy vegetarian male. The topic would always open a can of perma-competition from the others but would also open a healthy and honest dialogue. Mostly though, it was understood and accepted as one of the more amusing things about Elder Staples.

As a modern side note, there were anecdotal studies in the 2019 Louie Psihoyos documentary "Game Changers" which showed that a plant-based diet immediately increases the frequency and duration of nocturnal erections in men. So there is no wonder that a 19 year old male in the prime of his life on a plant-based diet would experience this. Being the brunt of the joke was taken in stride, but it would have helped to have been armed with the facts of how natural it all was. If only Game Changers would have been available in the late 1990's!

At 19 years of age, he lasted for the first 18 months without engaging in this forbidden practice. After that, he didn't care to try to avoid it much. Maybe it was due to the stressful period of disobedient companions and interrupted sleep patterns, or maybe his body finally won the battle over his obedience. In any regard, after eighteen months, he succumbed to occasional masturbation. He discovered that it relieved the tension and aggravation about sleep disruption and arguments with the other elders. He realized that there is a lot more to sound, quality sleep and perfect obedience than meets the eye. His disobedient fellow missionaries taught him much about sleep, diet, thalamus and masturbation with hardly a word uttered of any of these, except of course for the latter. There were plenty of comments and references and some late-night jokes about it from the other three missionaries while he tossed and turned past 10:30 PM, trying unsuccessfully to be obedient and get to sleep on time.

He struggled with the ingrained guilt associated with the practice of masturbation, even if he only did it occasionally. He felt depressed, unworthy and he found it very difficult to continue his missionary work. He felt discouraged, adopting an attitude of *Why try? I can't wait to get home and just start over.* It was a good thing he was near the end of his two-year service. He noticed that the jokes and comments by the other elders increased. Apparently, they had begun the practice also. Stress? The lack of sleep was beginning to affect them in unseen ways as well. This topic would certainly make for intriguing scientific studies, correlating veganism, virility, testosterone, sleep, and oh yeah, mental health.

Armed with education and facts it is now essential to open a healthy dialogue in the form of having honest discussions about this shamed and very misunderstood practice.

Post Mission

He concludes his mission honorably and returns home in 1999 from his two year service in Eastern Canada at which point he was prepared for the second chapter of his life. In Mormon culture, this consists of going to school, starting a career, getting married and starting a family. So, upon returning home, what does he do? Why, start college and look for a wife of course.

He loved the idea of getting married. It is one thing he wanted more than almost anything else. As a young lad in his early 20's, he gives this topic a lot of energy. Not only does he strongly look forward to the romantic idea of having a forever companion always and forever loving, warm—to him it sounds like heaven on earth, but it also meant that he could finally release his sexual tension, since only after marriage is it allowed. He wouldn't have to feel guilty about masturbation any longer. After all, why would he ever need to do it again when he is finally able to marry the girl of his dreams where they are the healthy outlet for each other, which is taught as the only way: no masturbation. No sex until marriage. The race against their hormones is on for all young men ages 12-24 until they can find someone suitable for marriage.

In the fall of 1999 while working at PetSmart, he met a promising prospect, another PetSmart employee. She was cute, smart, she laughed at his silly jokes, she liked animals. In every way, she seemed like the one—the only pebble in his way, which was actually a giant boulder is that she was Catholic. He wanted a temple marriage. After all, in Mormon culture, that is all that there is. Civil marriage is "less than", and a return missionary would not even consider anything other than marriage in the LDS temple.

He dated this wonderful girl for a few years. Yes, a few years. They have fun doing what young couples do. They watch movies; enjoy picnics and walks in the park, hiking with his big dogs. They laugh together, enjoy hot kissing sessions. She was a good sport and would even spar around with him some with his martial arts! They found that they had something special. They had an excellent chemistry. They "got" each other. Like him, she was the youngest of her siblings. They were in love and they realized just how comfortable they were with each other. It was beautiful and special. He had hopes. He had doubts. She attends church with him several times, and he attends a few Catholic masses with her family. Even an elder and trusted friend in his church told him that he should just marry her. "Just do it. She seems like the one for ya, Owen," he said plainly.

But to him, there was no other way other than rigid obedience. Everything would work out if he just insists on a temple marriage, no compromises. To do anything contrary is less than the best. He had been ingrained with this all of his life since his young days of Junior Sunday School. He was bound and determined to bring her to the fold; stay chaste; marry her the way he was taught, and enjoy happily ever after—in that order. That was his desire and was the only option worth considering. He had his girlfriend; now it was onward toward living the dream! He only needed to convince her that she need only do a few things first to be in good standing and get baptized...

The terrorist attacks of September 11th, 2001, strongly affected him. He was in shock and was angry—anger to the point of many tears. He knew that the entire nation was in mourning. He was mourning with them. His sweet girlfriend called him. They greet each other solemnly through the phone. He was slightly annoyed because there wasn't much to say after such a tragedy, and he was not in the mood for light conversation. Little did his immature mind realize that she was feeling it too. After a long silence, she managed to say: "I can't believe this." He agreed, with few words.

She came over to his house that night. He needed her and she needed him. They didn't say much. They watched a movie to escape everything. After the attacks, the hours and days blurred together. He knew he needed special care. He didn't feel like socializing or light talk; still, he sensed he needed people, especially at such a time. He had her. At such a time they say little, but at least they are together.

They expressed concern about the future and how this catastrophe would change everything. They speculate, discuss, and together are concerned and worried. They both wondered how this would affect the economy and the entire world; theories and rumors spread like a wildfire. He became afraid for the future adding to his fearful thinking. At least he didn't have to go it alone; he had her. It was naïve immaturity on his part that he didn't realize what a comfort she was to him at that time.

Together, late on a weekday evening, they went for a walk. He had a lot on his mind. Even in Utah, the only church open in town at that hour was an old Episcopal church with walls made of rocks within walking distance of where he'd grown up. He always liked the old look of the building itself and visited its grounds often as a child. In fact, they passed by the church often on their walks with his dogs and always enjoyed its nice, quiet grounds. But he'd never been inside of it. He wanted to go inside for some solace and comfort. She supported this desire, and together, they stepped inside through two propped open doors. It felt peaceful.

They discovered that they were alone inside the church. He took comfort in those open doors. At such a time, this Episcopal church trusted others by leaving the doors propped open even at night for people who seek to ease their pains, and to "mourn with others who are mourning" –Book of Mormon. They were quiet and said very little. He was reverent and still, although she felt the need to tell him to show some respect and refrain from walking all the way up to the altar, which he was on his way to do, in an attempt to explore and discover whether they were truly the only ones inside the church.

He muttered, not understanding, but honored her request and stayed down by the congregational benches. The stillness brought gentle order to his inner turmoil. This left an indelible impression on him…

She supported him when he finally got his snake. At the time of being ill as explained in The Wellness Diaries, his reptiles were beneficial for his mental health. He bought a baby ball python. One night when she was waiting for him to finish his workout so that they could go out to eat and then watch a movie, his friend from high school dropped by unexpectedly. She was welcoming and pleasant to his buddy "Josh" and playfully told him to show him the snake. He admired this about her.

Later in 2002 after the storm of the schizophrenia diagnosis and meds, as mentioned in The Wellness Diaries, she still hung in with him, even visiting him where he worked at a small pet store. She was a catch. Even his boss, an extroverted, harmless and friendly older gentleman, commented to her, "You're Owen's girlfriend!? Ooh you're cute! Looks like he's a lucky man."

Finally, he convinced her to begin to "investigate" his faith, which was the initial step to converting. They met with the Mormon missionaries to hear the six discussions, or lessons, over a period of a few weeks. It wasn't long ago that he was doing the same thing as these missionaries, bringing the spirit of truth to assist in converting people. Without a doubt, he should be able to bring his own sweetheart into the fold. She heard the six Mormon discussions presented by the missionaries. Many were waiting on the decision, including the lovebirds themselves, friends and family, but in the end, it must be her decision. The anticipation was high. There was much at stake. There was much to do. His main desire, what he had waited for all his life–a temple marriage was finally almost here!

They continued to have talks and debates even stark disagreements about the faith. She said things about the church that he couldn't quite understand. One of these was that they were organized more like a business, even their masses. (the LDS equivalent to Catholic Mass is called sacrament meeting). This frustrated and even angered him. His attitude was *"How can you argue with the truth?"*

Hindsight is better than foresight and he now sees what she meant. Part of him still wishes he could deny it, but he cannot.

She decided that the Mormon Church was not for her. He cannot convince her otherwise, and the spirit of truth couldn't either. He could not believe it. He had tried with everything he had. How?! She held to her decision and he held to his. She was every bit as stubborn as he was. He loved this about her. But not this time. The only way then was to part. This they did. That painful breakup took place on New Year's Day, 2003. This was heartbreaking by itself. Still, they managed to hang on for quite some time, getting together occasionally for a movie, or to talk on the phone. His rigid adherence to principles in which he so thoroughly believed caused him agonizing emotional pain—the irony....

Being without her warmth and affection was painful enough by itself. Then, on March 11th, 2003, the last time he would hear her sweet voice on the phone, she told him that she was with another. The pain at this point compounded a hundred-fold and he was not confident in his ability to bear it. Being without her, without her warmth was already much worse than he had anticipated; but then the pain was compounded by the knowledge that she was with another man at which point the pain and jealousy he would describe as debilitating, raw, exquisite and absolutely excruciating. His emotional heartstrings and logic crossed like two wires on a machine that were never supposed to touch. But touch they did, and they remained touching for some time—well into 2003 when things became unbearable and led him to try a new medication at the end of that March as discussed in The Wellness Diaries.

Still, he held firm to his faith and to his decision. His rigid hyper-religiosity with intent to listen to and heed everything taught by modern prophets of the LDS faith, including that a temple marriage is the only way to celestial glory brought him all the way back to square one.

His pain, his struggle, continued for an entire year. After a year, he got the idea to write her a letter. He still held out hope. He told himself, *What if they broke up?* While the chances may be slim, what if there is a chance? Several months passed by even into summer. His good friend noticed his deep gash and offered to call her on the phone to gain some insight and understanding. (You know the type of friend, the amazing kind that will do such things for another friend). He watched on pins and needles as his friend Steve walked around the backyard, conversing with her on the phone. He conversed with her for quite some time. She was kind, open and very communicative. The friend explained that Owen was just beside himself and he was worried about him, and that he was trying to help Owen acquire the needed closure. After the phone call ended, his friend, having realized that she had moved on, tried to console him and help Owen to accept it.

Apparently, Owen couldn't believe him. Months passed by. He gave it some more thought. He couldn't accept it and he couldn't believe it. Around winter of 2004, not long after his momentous job landing at the hardware store, he decided to hand write her a letter. He knew he simply must try; he must communicate. In the letter he explained that he had been dealing with his own demons and diagnosis of which she was aware and was so supportive about; he recognized that he was very rigid about religion; he told her he was being eaten alive by this, having taken for granted what he had, and that he now has high hopes but no expectations since he didn't know what was happening in her life. He finished the letter and although he could hardly believe it, he sent it.

Now there was no turning back. Although he realized that it may hurt terribly, reopening the wound that was still raw, he knew that the answer, whatever it may be, would help provide some closure. For the first few days after sending the letter, he felt depressed all over again, having relived all their memories with the wound still gaping. Even his boss at the hardware store noticed, attempting to greet him warmly with a "good morning." He appreciated the intent, but at the time it was cold outside, early in the morning and he felt no warmth. He felt awful.

Shortly thereafter a letter arrived in his parents' mailbox. He was rather surprised that she replied at all, but he was touched and grateful. As he read the words that brought both comfort and an exquisite, crushing throb, he had the closure he needed. It came on like a searing hot iron through his flesh into his core. She was still with the same man, and they were soon to be married. She expressed kind words of forgiveness and understanding, that she knew religion was important to him at the time. She acknowledged that she was also unbending, and that she should have been more patient in allowing his path to flourish. She even gave him words of encouragement that someday he would make some girl very happy. Near the end of the letter she said that this was the last correspondence he would receive from her and she wished him the best.

As compassionate, sweet and selfless as her reply was, it only angered and embittered him. It worsened the pain beyond comprehension. His thinking at the time was, *How could she have a fuller glass and be so spiritually alive than I am when she is not of the "true church"?* She was finishing her tech college degree and life was blossoming for her. *How could this be?*

He recalled the voice of an LDS leader at what is called a "fireside", presented by the institute of religion on the college

33

campus he attended in 1999. The talk was about sexual immorality, a very common topic in the LDS church, always spoken of with heaviness, dread, and fear of hell fire and damnation. The leader issued a warning to men— "priesthood holders". The only words he recalls was the warning that if sexual immorality is left unchecked and unheeded, "your world will go up in flames."

He was emotionally immature during his early college days and dating, (1999-2003) but he didn't want his world to go up in flames, so he thought maybe he should get married while he could still maintain his self-control, so that he could finally lose his virginity and do it right. If he did this, everything would work out. The table then was finally set for the LDS temple marriage he was brought up to want, his first marriage of 2005 as discussed in the first memoir, The Wellness Diaries.

The irony of this marriage was that it lasted only four months. Just before the two left on their honeymoon to consummate their marriage, and finally lose their virginity to each other, he needed to go to his parents' basement to make sure all the reptiles were fed prior to leaving. For this, he was seen as crazy and having something wrong with him. In his mind though, he had waited twenty-seven years, what was another two hours?

Everything he ever wanted, or thought he wanted, from childhood to middle age had its roots in his wanting to give and receive love. But it always left. Everyone he knew went away in the end. He still has warm memories of his mystery Catholic girlfriend and he realizes that he has a great deal of respect for her.

Summarized, what a trail he blazed and what a web weaved. He spent the next decade and a half putting all the pieces together…

CHAPTER 3

"What in the World Man"?
(2011-2016)

We now return to more recent times—where we left off after leaving his job at the hardware store in 2011. He then had much free time and his fair share of expenses with only 401K money that he had begun saving at his job since he was first hired there, believing at the time that the hardware store was to be his final destination of employment for life.

To make the dimes and dollars stretch for as long as possible, he was very frugal with money, even walked and often cycled his way to buy groceries with a basket on the back of his bike. Insurance, house payment and utilities still had to be paid. He himself didn't have health insurance after he left his full-time job. Fortunately, being a young vegan who also lived lightly on the earth, he didn't really need it. Health-wise, he was okay for those three years. He didn't have to go to the doctor during that time frame of 2011-2014, and he had only had two cavities in his whole life. For the next three years between his plant-based diet and his physical activity including any combination of bike, bus and boots, he was fantastically healthy. In fact, he felt like a superhero; he felt like he could do anything. That is, with only one exception—he was having real difficulty convincing anyone to hire him, the main thing that he so desperately needed!

It was a harsh reality that his ability to get a job was directly linked to his ability to hold on to his marriage, his home and everything shared by him and his queen.

This was just the beginning too. After he left the hardware store, he had plans to keep up the good vibes, as he was turning in job applications for at least a temporary cushion. Being the metropolitan area of downtown Ogden, the opportunities seemed endless. Surrounding stores in malls, other nurseries, even seasonal jobs at Halloween stores all saw his application and resume. He was confident that he could land *something, anything* at least temporarily (except Wal-Mart, or McDonald's to which he refused to apply), which would help to bring some income.

He volunteered at a wildlife rehabilitation center for a season to take his mind off of the stress of lacking money, as he lived on his 401K for the bare essentials and as he waited for calls on jobs. He was walking and riding his bike to and from the grocery store and also to where he volunteered, all of it some distance away. It took twenty-five minutes to walk to the store each way, or about five minutes on the bike. During this time, he also began a very small indoor plant maintenance business from his bike called "Botanist on A Bike". It brought a few fun gigs of income, and was excellent experience, but it didn't pay the mortgage.

During that summer there he was with his reusable bags, trekking to the grocery store with his newfound state of well-being. Little did he realize at that time just how utterly alone in this he was. There were no neighbors, members of the community, or friends, at least not at this time and place, who were prepared to join him in his new state of plant-based well-being and healthy lifestyle. No one in his circle was ready to join him, neither was his queen yet prepared to make those dietary and lifestyle changes.

With his basket on the back of his mountain bike that held a maximum of fifteen pounds he rode each week to stock up on vegan groceries from a health food store. (He hasn't shopped at Wal-Mart since 2003 out of principle, so that place, which was closer, was not an option). The health food store was the closest grocery store, but it was exorbitantly expensive. The next closest would be less expensive, but it passed several busy roads, including one of the busiest roads in the entire state of Utah. The next closest was a forty-minute bike ride each way, and one risks their own life trying to get there in a car, let alone on a bike!

Needless to say, he obtained his groceries from the closest health food store where the organic russet potatoes were $1.09 per pound! He didn't necessarily need organic potatoes, but being a health food store, for better or worse, the more expensive organic produce was all that was available. In the end, with more bills being due than money coming in, his mode of living was akin to constantly trying to clip and stretch pennies.

During this challenging time, he had one reprieve throughout the day, and that was the beautiful nature trail by the river within walking distance of his condominium. There was a path that followed the river for pedestrians; anyone walking their dog, rollerblading, cycling or skating was welcome on this beautiful nature trail. He spent significant time there daily and was deeply comforted by it. It taught him more about everything in life than almost anything else he'd experienced. It became his essential water. He learned that currently all other water with man-made influence is contaminated. There was no replacement for being with the birds, trees, ducks all beside the beautiful river. It became the finishing touch on his awakening, his becoming. He knows it is a sacred place.

Over the next few months, he turned in literally hundreds of applications to various stores near his house. Surely, he would land something. There are so many options within walking distance of his house. He also enjoyed his volunteer work helping to rehabilitate wildlife for successful release through the summer after he left the hardware store, into autumn and winter.

During the winter, he waited for his beloved queen to come home with the car each day. Once or twice a week they would take the car together to buy some food to eat throughout the week. This became a fond memory to him. He grew to love the two of them going to the grocery store together; it felt cozy, and it meant food in the fridge and in the kitchen. Since he was no longer away from home all day every day, he had more time with her during this snapshot in their history than during their entire marriage.

The Job Interview...

It becomes easy to deny one's authentic self and suck up to the sleaze in word and deed to get what one needs. The interviewer expects perfect eye contact to land the job regardless of rules of respect or other cultural norms that may not agree. John Doe could tell the interviewer that he had bone cancer but has since recovered; the interviewer would hardly bat an eye. But God forbid that Owen should mention his recovery from mental illness; to do so is to remain jobless. Yet, during the interview, there was no easy and tactful way of saying: "I have recovered from a mental illness." Our culture attempts to perpetuate its mores and norms that don't make sense in the first place because they are rooted in falsehoods and irrational absolutes. *The current cookie cutter system doesn't work for everyone.* We are gone all day from our shelter so that we can afford to live there, or at least to sleep there occasionally. We work in unnatural conditions, beneath fluorescent lights, sedentary for eight hours, doing repetitive work, using our bodies as a machine. We are stressed, overworked, and sick from diseases of western affluence. We keep going. We call it life, this 9-5 until 65 to pay off our shelters to then die a few years later from avoidable diseases brought about by stress, artificial un-whole food and over work of the past 30 years spent paying off the shelter. This is insanity, (mental illness?) but this is "normal" because western society (Capitalism) is based on this detrimental model.

From 2009 to 2014 he and his queen had it all in their new home by the river. They had all they ever needed to live happily ever after.

That is, except one key component: a guarantee to keep their shelter through thirty years of income to make mortgage payments. Having a place to live is an important aspect of any happy relationship and was at the very cornerstone of their lives. Relationships are healthier and happier when there is a secure place to live. The lack of which is a legitimate threat to a couple's very survival.

They made the same mistake everyone else does which was to sign a contract, a "guarantee" that they will spend the next thirty years paying off their shelter, at which point it would be 'theirs' so long as they continued to pay taxes on it. It worked for the first few years, but thirty years is a long time.

One needs a guaranteed job, but that is a lie; there are no guarantees, especially concerning jobs. In America it's all business. Jobs, struggles, promotions, personal disasters, layoffs come and go, especially with no college degree. Jobs are as fleeting as the media. How would it be to realize that in the end, the king has no say in his kingdom? His kingdom may be small, but at least it is his, right? Well, not so much.

This was the very painful lesson that he had to learn. All the love and strength he could muster up to impress his queen and compel her to not go elsewhere was just an illusion. It was an illusion that his own mind and strength alone could keep these things. The current structure of society made him weaker not stronger. His clawing, fighting and grasping at straws to hold on to what was "his", in the end, only weakened him. In a society based on a few lies that everyone breathes, he was powerless. The prince of their Sherwood, the romantic scene of a beautiful life with a cute little house and everything that they had built up, 'living the dream', he could not hold on; he could not keep it. The dream became a nightmare.

He tried with all his might, giving it everything he had to hang on. He slowly and painfully learned this lesson: that it was futile. There was more happening than met the eye. It was just under the surface, barely undetectable and largely in the dark. He soon reached the cold realization that it would all collapse. He was the timeless farmer in an industrialized brick, mortar and digital world. He was one person amidst the old rusty factory, a diseased and structurally unsound society. He could see it; others could not. Some unseen force at the top had him like a puppet on a string and knew him as a number only. He was just a dust particle in the giant vacuum. The modern king of his queen, in a day where almost everything is an option, getting a job—the one missing puzzle piece—was not an option! "How in the world was it true?!" The prince of Sherwood realized that he had no say, despite all his rants to stop the giant caterpillar from munching;

The caterpillar will continue to munch. The caterpillar is designed to only consume into oblivion—munching. The caterpillar has a disorder, the design has a flaw. Since it is not exposed to real light, the light of all creation, the caterpillar munches... and munches, but never morphs into a beautiful adult, which is designed to drink nectar. So, the munching continues. It will always continue. The caterpillar never reaches adulthood. There were too many caterpillars.

The puppet master counts on this. The puppet master of our sick society is above politicians, leaders of nations, banks, mortgages and gas prices. The puppet master owns all of these. Annual profits of any of these are pocket change for the puppet master.

All the frustration, anger, and intention to take care of business, pay the mortgage, and earn a buck to pay the HOA did not reach the real issue, because the real issue was larger than all of these. That is the point. The puppet master prefers to work secretively in darkness, anonymously, because it is known that if brought to light, the unethical works would be violently opposed by those who are enslaved. By the time he saw it, it was too late. He and his queen were merely a part of the puppet show and the collapse had already begun.

From bottom to top, this vacuum-society built on greed, continued to encroach, munching on already sick, weak, outdated structures, and a few carefully wrapped lies. This is the great illusion because it appears that we are in charge but it denies that mother nature is in charge, not us. This giant man-made vacuum, although clever in its design, is the great evil, the corporate Babylon. It will devour everything in its path. It has lost all sense of humanity. It is a system, a collective machine of mass-delusion more than any one individual or corporation.

He was bitter of the fact that the mortgage, HOA, the puppet master and even his queen's coworkers had more say in *their marriage* than did he and his queen. Were they powerless? No, but they were beyond saving it too. His anger, frustration and stress were all due to fighting for his queen and their home. His voice was given no merit. These people can't see The Well; they have yet to taste of The Spring. They couldn't see him. They could only see *parts* of his plans and sensibility. Their minds were made up. They all witnessed firsthand his happy, blissful state after going vegan. But they dismissed it; some even say that it was just a temporary high. He was perceived as being crazy. "Oh. See, I told you, he needs to get back on his meds."

The backbiting, the assumptions, judgments, gossip and guessing games began, and they continued long and hard. They took their toll. They essentially turned against him, fighting him for confidence, support and good vibes, the very fuel he needed to make things happen, to *keep* what was his! He was treated like the enemy; the enemy of what exactly?! How blind can people become? These things all culminated in the likelihood of his losing everything he had and everything he loved—his house, his wife, their family of animals. Just how okay with "the way things are" was he expected to be?

Then, one day out of the blue he finally landed a job interview. Wow, really are you serious? Yes, it was true. He managed to schedule a job interview with a large grocery store chain that wasn't Wal-Mart. He heard good things about working for them.

"Yes, we're serious. We're going to give you the chance to demonstrate to us your professional credentials and amuse us via a thirty second commercial, "sing-and-dance style", during this interview. We know you're nervous, so we'll watch carefully... Go."

"How honest can I be?"

"We want to hear it all."

"Oh, I bet you do; (wink) so since you insist, here goes: I am quirky but have a heart of gold. My word is all you will ever need from me in terms of honesty and dependability. Shred the contracts, in fact don't use the trees or ink to print them in the first place. I will look at you when you are talking to me, but honestly, it's not very comfortable for me. I see you, and I am listening whether making eye contact or not. It probably has more to do with the small Thalamus, and the accompanying automatic compensation that must take place. That is, with a smaller Thalamus, a person's sleep world must be larger to compensate. Yes, an annoying amount of energy must be spent to get enough sleep each night. Since I don't use a mechanical, digital, or electric alarm, I rely on my internal one, and it is perfectly accurate..."

In spite of his reassurance that he was a human with a good heart, honest and dependable with a well-adjusted sleep schedule to accommodate his smaller Thalamus, he knew already that it is the robotic G.Q personality in line immediately after him that would get this job. For Mr. or Mrs. G.Q. it was merely a job, and he'll only have to be so-so honest, or so-so golden each day, just enough to impress the right people and to put on a show. He had nothing invested in this and was merely going through the motions. He can live a lie because he doesn't care about much. That is, Mr. G.Q. was just honest enough to not get caught, after that, he can play on his cell phone, multi-tasking when the bosses are talking to him, not really listening to the customer because the customer is probably also multi-tasking and isn't really paying attention; G.Q. will do it because he can. These types do the bare minimum, just enough to squeak by.

Meanwhile, Owen will listen to the customer simply because it is a fellow human being talking, then of course there's the eye contact thing. The customer wonders how well he really listens, since he is listening so well, that his eyes go slightly out of focus in order to catch the overall essence of what is actually being said as not to be overwhelmed by unnecessary detail, enabling him to *actually* listen *and* hear them fully. How about that–and he learned it on his own. Have G.Q figure that one out. Ha!

"Thanks for your time. We'll be in touch."

He knows the interviewers won't contact him. There's your thirty-second commercial, your sound bite. Enjoy the lies, the hypocrisy, no ethics and the bare minimum from Mr. G.Q.

The interview didn't go so well. The above is only a slight exaggeration, but he didn't get the job. Instead, he was pained and felt like he had betrayed himself and was willing to pretend to be something he was not, to grovel and beg, live a lie to earn a buck. It reaffirmed his poverty, both in lifestyle and in his person.

The Oasis in the Desert

Early in that new year of 2012, he hit the applications straight on, polishing up his resume' to the best of current standards, hoping for another interview, all to no avail. All the jobs, most of the Utah economy were further south in the Salt Lake valley—one of the most expensive places in the state to live, where one must practically earn six figures to reside there. Jobs (and good ones at that) were much less common in the Ogden area where he lived at the time in his Sherwood shelter with 30-year mortgage. It would stand to reason that with the hustling bustling downtown Ogden area that was within walking distance of his residence, there would be good jobs available. This was not the case, only retail and warehouse jobs were available. *Great! I'll take any of those, too.*

None of them replied.

Then, like a gift, *finally* that March he was hired to work at a nursery in west Layton. The location is some distance away—a twenty-five minute drive by car from his condo, but he and his queen were desperate for income. He knew he must go for it, and he jumped at the chance. They were still a one-car couple, and the nursery was far enough west that it was beyond all bus routes. His queen needed the car for her job. His only option was to take his bicycle on the State Street bus route (470) to the nearest stop in Layton, then get off with his bike and ride the great remaining distance west. He did this each way, each day. Sometimes when a long customer purchased thirty or more trees he stayed late, causing his strength to be zapped.

One night, he helped a customer who bought several dozen trees. He missed his usual bus and was delayed by more than forty-five minutes and didn't catch the bus until well after dark. More than anything, he wanted to get home to his queen. When he finally arrived home, his queen was rightfully stressed and worried about his long delay, the odd hours of the seasonal job, and the distance traveled on bike/bus to get there. He was stressed also. He knew that it was not an ideal setup for getting to and from work, but it was the only option they had given the circumstances. It all added up to more tension and stress, not less.

From this nursery, often he clambered his bike onto the rack of the bus well after dark, then after a forty-five minute bus ride where he must ride his bike the remainder of the way home. He talked to people all day, having spent the day outside in the sun, lifting shrubs, trees and bags of mulch. Maybe he should have packed more calories with him. Cliff bars were quite expensive to eat each day when they were barely able to make their mortgage payment as it was. At the end of his work shift, he would already be spent and exhausted, to then have to muster the strength to ride his bike several miles to catch the bus.

Bills were due. There was life, dental, and health insurance; these would all be due throughout the month. Further, together they had student loans, animals, car insurance, not to mention the mortgage. The Homeowner's Association had continued to increase its monthly rate ridiculously until it became like a second mortgage. This combined with all the other reasons, led them to fall behind on their monthly payments to the HOA, which was ceaselessly a hungry bottomless pit. Things were tight and it was a constant struggle trying to figure out new ways to clip or stretch a penny.

The job at this nursery was seasonal, so in June 2012, in what seemed like reliving the great depression of the 1930's, he was released from his employment. They were already just scraping by, and now what had been the oasis in the desert seemed a mere mirage. The nursery had at least brought in a paycheck every two weeks, but with no extra financial cushion, he and his queen were feeling the pinch in less than two weeks after the nursery employment ended.

During the middle of summer, they were again standing with hands in the air since he was again unemployed. He was at least eligible for unemployment at this point. As long as he turned in his four applications per week (via bus, bike and boots, and of course online if they could continue to afford internet service) he would receive his $140 per week. He could not pay the mortgage or sustain himself on that, let alone his queen and family of animals.

There he was—one person doing exactly what much of America does. Except for the very wealthy, many can relate living paycheck to paycheck, working as hard as humanly possible, but still falling further and further behind. One looks up and will likely think: "There has *got to* be a better way."

Yes, there is indeed a better way. When humans turned their backs on the earth, it was a digression. The quality of our treatment of the earth began to diminish. This was so gradual that we didn't notice. Throughout most of human history, there were forests, clean air and water in abundance. Few were considering how to conserve when there was what seemed like a limitless supply. But since the industrial revolution, acquiescing to nature and living in alignment with its bounds is what humanity has missed through what we call "progression". We only see this now in the 21st century when there is only a little nature left and even less time to fix it.

By the end of the summer, there he was again unemployed, having turned in more than two-hundred applications since spring around the bustling retail sector of South Ogden. With a myriad of businesses and seemingly endless opportunity, he landed only four. For all his filed applications, it seemed like he should have had more interviews. He figured out the most likely reason for this: The dates shown on his resume' were puzzling to prospective employers because they could see that he was then 36 years of age, but had no college degree, very little experience (beyond animals and plants) for his age, and yet no felonies or criminal record. They were unable to piece it all together in order to understand his unique situation, and in today's busy world of "business as business" in America, nobody has the time to do so. Everything he did and was (recovery from mental illness, therapy and meds, the writing, botany,) required some real zooming in on the details to fully understand. After all, at first glance, it seemed like a fifteen-year haze; he essentially looked like a drifter although it was to the contrary! This fifteen-year detour that his life took was filled with much more detail than the average employer wanted to sift through, and nearly every single one of his two-hundred applications were undoubtedly tossed with hardly a second glance.

Who can blame an interviewer for not wanting to zoom in on all the details to understand his empty work experience? There was a lot that they did not know, and a lot that he was not prepared to sum up for them in the thirty second sing-and-dance commercial that one is expected to give during a job interview. How to summarize the ten-year detour that his life took (ten years at that time—the detour would last five more years) due to a medical condition—the mental illness from which he had recovered against all odds through a healthy lifestyle, including a plant-based diet, quality sleep and outside time with nature, bathed in natural light? He wrote books about this and a blog but mentioning this would only make him seem manic and further prevent employment. Neither could he say that this medical condition was a mental illness—and paranoid schizophrenia at that. There was and is still too much stigma attached to mental illness, and one would scarcely dare to say it during an interview. He was stuck between a rock and a hard place, with seemingly nowhere to turn.

With the mere handful of interviews that he did obtain, when asked what he had been doing with his time, he learned to come up with a memorized script that went like this: "My life took a ten-year detour due to a medical condition. I have since recovered and it is no longer an issue for me." But this was not enough. He was damned if he said mental illness. He was also damned if he withheld detail, merely saying, "medical condition." The singing and dancing weren't fancy enough. His telling them that he had been busily studying and learning on his own was not enough. The truth was too true. It was after the 190th job application, he was beginning to realize what was happening to his applications, and although he memorized and rehearsed the script very thoroughly, he realizes that it may not work in time. He took a cold, hard look at reality. It was looking like all of his momentous efforts, trekking, talking, and clawing would not land him a job in time to allow him to keep his home, his queen and their children of animals in Sherwood Park by the beautiful forest and river that was his haven. No employer cared to sift through those complicated details to decide whether to believe him. They would simply pass him by and move on to the next applicant. This is undoubtedly what they did.

This cycle of hardship was to continue for the next three years. He took any odd and temporary jobs that he could, (with many of them paying only minimum wage which was still at the time of this writing only $7.25 per hour) holding hope that his ship would come in, that his published books would start to catch on and sell or that he would land that special job, that tailor-made situation. These were high hopes while he had no college degree, no formal trade or training that could earn him a living wage. Many of these temporary jobs were in the middle of the industrial side of town, a virtual ghetto, where he would be doing production jobs for poverty wages, where literally his co-workers were people battling with addiction to heroin, felons, ex-convicts, people on bail and on and off homeless.

There was no chance to save money, no chance to go to school, no chance to get ahead—no hope. It was an endless cycle.

School was not an option at the time because he and his queen together "made too much money" to qualify for grants. Neither did they want to risk more debt by taking out student loans. As it stood already, each dollar earned was spent making ends meet and to fill the bottomless black hole with a garden hose. As soon as he earned fifty dollars, forty-eight of it was overdue somewhere in the overhead canopy of bills. The money was all tied up in the earning, the getting and the spending, particularly on the mortgage and HOA (which, remember, continued to increase). The health insurance, dental, car and home insurance, internet, phone, the car and gas; they could not continue. There was nowhere to turn; it was a dead end. There were long bouts of worry and stress mixed with cozier times where it felt like all would be okay. They needed some fun, some reprieve from the encroaching depression. He managed to scrape together enough cash for a night in Salt Lake City to see his favorite band, 311 in concert. His queen even endured the 311 concert with him; they made an outing of it. This was a much-needed, fun reprieve, but they had to return to the reality of the black hole of bills.

Throughout the carousel of temp jobs, time and time again he believed he was rescued by a job that seemed like "the one." It was always just a few cents per hour more than what he made before. In comparison, they seemed like gems and he felt rich. After a few years of living like this, he finally realized that he was only spinning his wheels getting nowhere. He watched good, "down home" small businesses grow to the point where they would incorporate and become part of the corporate matrix. He watched these companies go from small business with some flexibility room for employees, a family-like atmosphere with some wiggle room and mobility for each employee to a giant impersonal corporation, negating all semblance of the personal touch. They became a giant factory, robotic, whatever life-blood, heart and compassion that remained was swallowed up in the building of the gigantic factory—one that was designed for only one thing—limitless growth. It is a fallacy that continuous unceasing growth is ideal.

Seriously? Is this for real? You know this sounds familiar; of course, it does. This is us. This is America. It is we the people working for what we call a living. It is all the time and energy spent in the earning and buying, the getting and the spending, but getting nowhere as we claw our way up that slippery slope. Minimum wage is still $7.25 per hour in the U.S. Many of us work two, three, or even four jobs just to try to stay afloat. We only get on average two weeks of vacation time per year. Many European countries get up to six weeks. Entry level jobs without a degree might pay around $10-12 per hour, but of course, many jobs pay only minimum subsistence wage. Much of the country's dollars are caught up in healthcare ("disease-care") and the pharmaceuticals industry—the richest 1% of the nation's population. The current setup allows this and industries like it to largely avoid paying taxes. It is easy to see why a shift is needed, and why this cannot continue. As the middle class continues to shrink, there will be increasing poverty, homelessness, slum conditions and an increase in urban 'food deserts' which everyone pays for as these spread like a cancer in the wealthiest country on Earth.

At Least This Oasis in the Desert Has a Fountain

In April of 2013, he somehow managed to convince one more place to give him a chance. They even saw his blog and he was still hired! Cactus and Tropicals of Salt Lake City picked him up. There was light at the end of the tunnel. It was a seasonal position in the heart of Salt Lake City, much farther south where the economy was stronger, but very far from his home. All other job prospects were rather grim; but at least it was a job, and it was a job that he loved. He enjoyed the atmosphere of again being outside with the plants, trees, shrubs, birds and insects. He also really liked the customers and the people he worked with...

This is what it is like trying to find employment and a livable situation for someone who, at any time of their life was diagnosed with a mental illness. Even when it is part of their past, they are basically branded for life. They then spend much energy deciding ever so carefully who is told, and how much is told. Mental illness still has a negative stigma; not to mention the aftermath of what it is like for someone who makes such a wonderfully bold claim that improving their lifestyle has effectively treated it. It is that simple; but it is never allowed to be that simple. People generally expect complex answers and a cabinet full of meds, and the simple answer is dismissed.

Out of desperation, he took jobs which even at $10 per hour did not provide a living wage due to the ever increasing "cost of living" in the booming Utah economy. Even with their combined resources, they could hardly afford to afford housing; bills were due and there were mouths to feed. Each trip to the grocery store was one of anxiety and guilt for spending the gas to get there and for choosing to buy food out of the mortgage budget.

The irony of The Well is that in curing his Schizophrenia, the aftermath and stress of trying to find a job, trying to keep his love relationship and buy food, trying to keep his condo in Sherwood Park led to symptoms that resemble PTSD.

Being that his new job at Cactus and Tropicals was in the heart of the capital city of Salt Lake and he lived 50 miles to the north, he was again busing to work for the entire first year of his employment. The fastest mode of public transit, the Frontrunner train, was not conducive to the location, because to catch it, he would have to back track some distance, on foot or on bike. It was not feasible.

Like déjà vu, during the planting season he would leave his house at about five in the morning, walk twenty minutes (six blocks) to catch the bus, get on the bus, transfer twice, walk twenty more minutes (six blocks) from the bus stop to arrive at work three and a half hours later. He often was gone from his shelter for more than sixteen hours, having worked his eight-hour shift and then took the same route home after work. He often got home after ten o'clock at night, at which time he prepared his vegan meal, water and snacks for the next day, showered alone if there was time, only to get up and do it all again the next day.

His workdays were enjoyable in the sun, and there was fun even if it did ultimately accumulate to his utter exhaustion. Being in the sun all day every day is tiring. His commutes via bus to and from work (3.5 hours each way) were long and arduous. He brought books to read. Still, he rarely saw his queen, although sometimes her schedule permitted her to meet him outside with their small dog as he walked from the bus stop to their home around 10:30 pm.

He knew they needed more, so he continued to turn in applications of course. There was still the hope of landing that job right in the area of where he lived, (which would be ideal and would make the most sense and would at least theoretically save them from losing it all,) with the myriad of businesses and opportunity just down the road. That is why he did it all again, reapplying to most of them, still to no avail. He couldn't convince them to hire him. His applications likely met the fate of all the others and were not given a second glance.

Through the fall and winter of endless job searching, he was trying to maintain a positive energy of attraction to avoid appearing desperate to employers. Upon being asked by several people in their mutual circles how the job search was going, he had to face the look of worry and uncertainty on the face of his queen.

During this time she was regularly asked about his job situation by her coworkers. The women who worked with his queen tended to talk about personal, private things. He noticed this as one of the major differences between men and women. Women get together for more substantial, personal talk. Men get together for guy talk, mostly rambunctiousness and some form of competition; he has heard a phallic reference to this as a 'sausage fest'. Maybe these are annoying to others because men get blamed for being all brawn and no brain, too much testosterone, activity and rough play. Men experience a collective disorder in the form of pissing contests and ego-stroking, perhaps resulting from the childhood game of sword fighting with urine, rough play and boob jokes! This is what makes men men. If this is men's collective disorder, then women's collective disorder is excess chat and gossip. Chatting and gossip alone are fine—it makes women women. There is no doubt that women are better communicators than men. However, he drew the line at backbiting. The nasty backbiting was the beginning of problems. This became hard for him to stomach. The Right View, and Right Speech, and time spent in silence found in Buddhism is an excellent antidote to this toxic tendency. Regular fasting of Christianity is another effective remedy.

He supposed it is a human need to organize thoughts and activities somewhat so that focus can be directed to other things. Women need consistency from men on some things, but in others it only annoys them. He only reads minds *sometimes*. What was a poor guy with no formal vocational training to do? He was so utterly stuck between a rock and a hard place and everyone got to comment and glare at him about it.

The backbiting, assumptions and speculation all caused damage; all of it became traumatic. The more attached to his queen and Sherwood he became, missing her and his home so much from being away from them for 16 hours a day, the more slippery they all became. He could not get a firm grasp on them. The questions, the reminders, the opinions from others shoot him at rapid fire. They pop up, and stack. These questions and opinions from everyone in their circles of what they all think he should be doing led to misunderstanding, family feuds, tension, resentment and plenty of money arguments.

If only his queen could have realized how outside of himself he was due to his utter frustration of being so impossibly stuck; the frustration of realizing that they as a couple had no say in their own life and that this was just part of the illusion, the lie.

He now sees that at that time he was emotionally immature. If only his queen could have known this, leading to some understanding that he was at the time, entirely unprepared to handle such an onslaught, meteor shower of financial stress, stacking bills, employment uncertainty and finally, backbiting and resistance from others. He recalls his own foolish mistakes such as hogging the clothing closet for one of his snakes and limiting the number of books kept in the bedroom to improve Feng-Shui in the home. Hindsight is better than foresight.

For men, spending time and energy on processing emotion is quite new. He later learns in his Human Sexuality course that men's and women's brains are quite different. Particularly noteworthy is the greater thickness of the Corpus Callosum (broad band of nerves) in women's brains compared with that of men. This increases bilateral activity of the left and right hemispheres of the brain[1] (Smith et al., 2005. Crooks and Baur Our Sexuality, 12th ed.). He concludes that women are generally more emotionally mature than men are and, if this is a biological fact, then men deserve to be given a break.

How was he to know that recovery from his schizophrenia would lead to such a storm of circumstances and would uncover an emotionally immature man in which the hail storm led to PTSD? After all he had overcome, after beating the odds, one would think life would be smooth sailing. The irony was the stunted growth, like a light-deprived plant, that was revealed *after* all that he had overcome.

He loved his newfound seasonal job at Cactus and Tropicals. It reminded him that he existed after all and he had an identity! But what about his being away from his home and queen for 16 hours a day during the season? Theoretically, this could be justified because it was at least a job, right? Sure; then again, being away for 16 hours a day for four months was a big deal, bigger than they realized. He loved the job, his coworkers, the hours, being outside again in the heart of Salt Lake City among the trees, shrubs, vines, bees and sunshine that he'd grown to love. It seemed like the answer, the dream, and in many ways it was! There was one part missing though: Where was his home and queen? They were always miles apart, always elsewhere, somewhere out there, away from the adventures and all the things she needed to see, which was everything he needed to show her to witness and sustain the newfound confidence in him, the good vibes that were so essential at the time. But she worked full-time too so they was always distance between them, being in two different parts of the state, all day every day, so they could afford to sleep in their two-bedroom shelter at Sherwood and rarely see each other.

The American Dream is supposed to be for keeps! The part he played in building a kingdom, as taught to him all his life by his religion, was not supposed to be a mirage! He was supposed to be able to keep it—all of it. The fairytale was supposed to have a happy ending. The American dream and the pursuit of life, liberty and happiness was supposed to make it possible for him to keep all those things, allowing him and his queen to live happily ever after, experiencing hard times, sure, but that would only add to the adventure and memories once they reached their "happily ever after".

As grateful as he was to have a permanent position (even if only seasonal), and with hopes of saving some money since he spent very little, his philosophy, his level of well-being and healthy lifestyle and the bliss of being outside and living simply could not be sustained given his current circumstances. His relationship with his queen could not continue to grow. The schedule and seasonal employment compounded by resistance from others was beginning to bring stress.

There was also the off season. After October, he again had no income until the short Christmas season with live Christmas tree sales. After Christmas, there he was again without income until about April when the season would start again. Things were at least manageable until winter; then they had many questions. Without his full-time benefits from the hardware store, neither of them had insurance. What if he or she was injured or gets sick? What do we do during the winter when he had no income?

The poverty was spreading into other areas of their life. The 3.5-hour bus rides each day began to add up. He was tired, worn out, exhausted, stressed and now his philosophy of taking care of the planet and saving money by living lightly on the earth was again challenged by the probability of having to buy a car to commute to work each day from Ogden to Salt Lake City. Cars are very expensive. On those wages he may be able to scrape up enough to buy a clunker, but in a few months of driving that distance each day, he would again be in the same boat when the clunker broke down. The only way would be to go into debt for a car, whether new or used. He knew better than to do this. Together they had taken Dave Ramsey's Financial Peace University, which they received as a wedding gift, so they had decided to avoid more debt at all costs.

He did not earn enough money, nor was he eligible for insurance due to being a part-time and seasonal employee. Neither was it an option to sell their condo in Sherwood to relocate closer to his work. As mentioned earlier, housing in Salt Lake City was and is prohibitively expensive and only those with a six figure annual income can afford to live in or near it. They had recently re-financed their condo which made their monthly payment $100 less. They were already living in the most inexpensive location possible and still struggled, so it was not an option to uproot and relocate to a more expensive area even if it was closer to his work.

He felt like a dog chasing its tail! His queen made quite a bit more money than he did having a degree, but she was in a financial bind with bills to pay also, and if they did relocate closer to Salt Lake City, it would then be her long commute to work.

Is a collapse coming? Well, is the sky blue?

Many readers will relate to this experience. This is exactly what has happened to so many people. It is time to ask questions. We are justified in this, to question authority, the establishment, the current setup, the rigged game. Seeing the disparities point blank are all too real.

The irony of The Well is that while he could see the golden stairway, the better way, the giant beanstalk that he could climb to heaven, he realized he was the only one who could see it. He realized it was his life's purpose to help others see it. The irony of The Well is that the diagnosis of mental illness, including the therapy, meds, the attempt to differentiate illusion from reality, the first eleven years, is only the *first half* of the battle. The *second half* came after recovery! Who would have ever thought that the people, places, and mostly the *habits* he had built up to that point from *reaction* to pain, fear and lack would be the second half of the battle?

The second half had yet to collapse right behind him, and he barely made it out before it did. The great fall does occur. The second half of his recovery has to do with leaving the giant factory/hospital, the structure of society that has outlived its usefulness and which needs major revision. The structure, the system is to blame; that, and the puppet master, the illusion, and the lies that he has bought into in an effort to survive and attain a basic level of happiness. The battle is a total of fifteen years, (2001-2016).

He still somehow managed to shoulder the exhaustion and maintain his seasonal employment at Cactus and Tropicals in Salt Lake City where he loved the people and the atmosphere for three years. He was beyond grateful to again be employed, and to confirm his existence and his identity; even if it was a part-time seasonal position where he returned each spring. At least it was something. Then again, there was the other big issue of being apart from his queen all day every day. They felt worlds apart. There was so much to do and see in Salt Lake City but he never had the money to show her these or do any of them. While he was there working, or from the long bus rides home he wanted to explore Salt Lake; he was constantly reminded of things that he would love for her to see but knew he would never have money, time, or energy to do so—not in his current circumstances.

During that three-year period at Cactus and Tropicals he took on another part-time job in a warehouse in North Salt Lake to cushion his seasonal employment for security. Since both jobs were in the Salt Lake area in the heart of Utah economy, he was still trying to get to work each day via bus. The job was at a printing warehouse that also did outsourcing for various other companies. He was usually involved in manufacturing and production. One of the main tasks was to assemble vitamin kits for another company. Since this was done by hand, there was an incentive called a "piece rate" to assemble vitamin kits quickly. The repetition made it easy to become good and really fast, so between his hourly wage of $8.00 and the piece rate based on how many kits he could assemble per hour, he averaged about $14 per hour, more than he'd ever made in his entire life. It looked like a nice cozy job to spend some time, shoot, possibly even his *life* since he could make so much! He liked his coworkers, and the job was not hard for the money he made. He basically got to pick his own schedule if he was consistent with it. In every way it looked doable.

He decided to stay at this position, even through the big collapse of everything he had. This included his marriage. He and his queen both agreed that they were spent and depleted, with no energy or motivation left to try to piece their situation back together. It has been said that no couple is the same after their first fight, and that money fights are among the most destructive. With mutual respect and love, they decided that they just couldn't continue as things were, and that divorce was their only viable option. He lost it all; his condo, his queen and some of their pets are no longer his...

At the end of the three years, despite being generously gifted through a family member with the clunker car that he'd considered earlier, he could not continue as things were. He was just too spent and deeply entrenched in poverty both monetarily and in well-being. He could not continue the farthest commute to Cactus and Tropicals on his current salary, either via bus or car, working in a rich neighborhood but living in a poor one nearly 50 miles to the north.

He hoped that his new warehouse job would act as a counterbalance to the pain of losing his home and his queen through divorce. He also had no option but to crash land and move into his parents' home in Clearfield where he was raised.

The crash occurs and it is merciless...

The Big Collapse (2014-2016)

There is a common expression among advocates of a healthy lifestyle. "Once you know what is behind the curtain, you cannot pretend that you do not know what is behind the curtain." [2]

As explained in The Wellness Diaries, after adopting a vegan diet with his new superhero suit, it was a step into refinement; he shed the excess in his life and developed an aversion to toxicity, be it environmental, social, or occupational.

This was largely unexplored territory and it was a continuous learning curve. His entire being (spirit, mind and body) then demanded some consistency, some rhythm to his schedule. The doctor's note had requested that he be allowed a schedule from 9-6 with no extreme or fluctuating hours. He had read many books about health and wellness, the environment and spirituality. He was confident of his path and knew what was taking place. He learned things by trial and error on his own in addition to what he had read. He got busy practicing and applying these concepts; it seemed that his learning and observations carried him to the farthest reaches of the universe. He had acquired a decent amount of knowledge about a wide range of topics. All these things he now knew helped him see how extremely beneficial and healing they would be for life on this planet for generations to come, but it was too early to be put into motion. Collective humanity was not prepared for them.

Put into motion through the right channels and model, this information would change the world. But since humans were not quite ready, things had to happen structurally on a global and societal level first to encourage the change. Unfortunately, he could not realize this while experiencing financial stress, which stressed his love relationship, his marriage. He had to take a short sale on his home at the same time he and his queen were filing for divorce at the end of 2014. He tried to sell it, but this was unproductive since they had recently refinanced. They had to settle for a short sale, and hopefully get at least a few hundred dollars out of it. The short sale fell through—twice. The only other options were foreclosure or bankruptcy. Ironically enough, it costs a lot of money to file for bankruptcy to pay an attorney to tell all included parties: "he's out of money." He opted for foreclosure. As though this wasn't hard enough to swallow, at the time of his having to move from there, he still owed $3,000 to the HOA. He asked them for forgiveness of the debt, or any wiggle room at all that they could allow. He wrote letters of hardship and made many phone calls. The HOA would not budge. There was no mercy. At the worst of his despair and heartache, having lost everything, he was forced to pay what he owed leeching precious minerals out of already bare bones.

Early in 2016, throughout the entire hardship of losing his condo through financial strain and his queen through divorce, he decided to take on full-time employment at the printing warehouse for insurance benefits, and to earn some extra money. It was not his passion; nor does it confirm his existence and identity like Cactus and Tropicals did, but he liked his coworkers; it was closer to his parents' house in Clearfield than Cactus and Tropicals and he made more money than ever before. He hoped to start over and rebuild his life. With more money than ever before ($14 per hour) it seemed to him like a good place to start doing it. Things appeared to be getting cozy and secure for him at last.

They say everything happens at once.

Very shortly thereafter he heard through the printing warehouse grapevine that they were eliminating the piece rate and also changing locations, moving to a much bigger building farther away in West

Valley City, with plans to expand and then incorporate. This was a hard blow. He communicated to his boss about his financial struggle of trying to figure out bus and gas money each day for the long commute, and how the piece rate was the only thing that made the wage livable, and how $8 per hour was not a living wage in Utah, hoping that something could be done. Thankfully he was grateful to see his boss stand up and act toward getting his raise. He got a big one, from $8 to $10 per hour.

With no piece rate, gone were the plush days with his fast kit assembly, $14 per hour, and flexible schedule. Yet his car, health insurance and 401k were all contingent on his working full-time at the printing warehouse. With little experience, he worked odd tasks, a worker in an industry he knew little about, with little passion invested in it, and no training, so he eventually excelled in the position of delivery driver. He felt torn because on one hand he enjoyed getting out on the road and seeing so much of the state. He delivered from Logan to Park City to Lehi and all over Salt Lake City, where he had always liked to explore. There were so many good restaurants and fun things to do, but again, there was no money to do them or anyone to enjoy them with after a divorce. No human is meant to drive for eight hours a day and then drive the 40 minutes back home each day. As much as he loved seeing the sites, driving all day every day could not continue.

We see that well-intending individuals from bottom to top only make up a portion of the hierarchy, and in the end their hands are also tied. These issues of increasing poverty, minimum wage locked at $7.25 per hour, a "disease-care" system that at least one documentary refers to as a 'poor design and irrational'[3] are rooted in greed with a large percentage of overall U.S dollars being tied up in the canopy of "disease-care" connected to big pharmaceuticals.

Consider the millions of "working poor" in the United States, working one or several jobs for $10 per hour or less. Due to the rising cost of living and stagnant wages, one can either pay rent or eat on $10 per hour. One simply cannot do both. Yet, when people "shack up" to make ends meet and combine resources and expenses they are ironically referred to as sinners by the hypocrisy of rich, white, greedy, Christian upper classes that create these discrepancies in the first place. These are problems within our social structure which is a monopoly of unbridled greed.

Shortly after the short sale of his condo, the divorce and crash landing at his parents' house, in desperation he even thought about joining a gang. He figured this was his only hope since he was permanently branded by his history of jobs, mental illness and failed relationships. The main thing that deterred him was knowing that he was not a gangster at heart; when it came down to it, he knew he could not go through with the required initiations or lifestyle to join a gang, but it demonstrates the utter hopelessness he was feeling.

These issues are indeed social problems. Many hands make light work. We can bring these issues to light through our greatest assets, namely communication, engaging in healthy dialogue and discussion, conscious living, education, knowledge, and awareness.

This is our current America. You know you relate. Just imagine what could be done to improve the lives of so many people as well as the fate of the earth if billions of U.S dollars were not tied up in the canopy of irrational disease-care. There would be enough for a more even distribution of wealth and power, without the bipolar extremes of domination by force and strangulation of the have-nots. More people would be in a position of having enough to keep their beloved queen in their Sherwood dream. Here's a fun comparison: the minimum wage in Australia is about $21 per hour. An unskilled worker can sling pizzas and they will be paid $21 per hour. Even factoring in the differences in cost of living, Australians enjoy a higher quality of life than the average American.

What he had been through, the awakening and the vision of the ideals that he sees is real. However, it was years ahead of the current state of things on earth, and very few people in his circles could see it. There were only a few; only enough to help him realize that he was indeed sane, but that it was simply too early. The dark ages were leading to the Renaissance, but what year or event marked the defining line? Was he years away, only months? For those living back then, who knew? Could the medieval mind have marked the Renaissance in that present time, or known at what point the new dawn could be? He thinks not.

PART 2

CHAPTER 4

Then... Abundance Flowed in Other Ways

"People with this schedule and lifestyle that he
found—being outside among plants, gardens
and life are called farmers, even peasants.

Have you ever had something that you just knew you wanted beyond anything else? This could be a tangible thing, or it could be a lifestyle, a situation, or to visit a certain place, but then you changed your mind after a few years of having it? This is because we think we know what we want, but we only see pieces. We don't fully know what it is that we want until we go full circle and see the whole picture, putting one's whole life into focus and seeing things from multiple perspectives.

There is no doubt about it, during his professional life he had spent much time outside regardless of season in the sun, rain and snow with the bees, ladybeetles, trees, birds and flowers. There are people who have spent this much time outside throughout most of human history. For the last several thousand years of human history people have largely been closely tied to agriculture, working hand in hand with plants and animals in villages and pastoral societies. Life was the opposite of the modern day. It could be said that we were outside based. Warehouses, skyscrapers and digital gadgets were not an option. But today, the few people who do spend that much time outside are farmers, peasants. They simply tend their plot of land, do their work and obtain food—farm to kitchen.

As for him, there were only a few options available in trying to be more attuned to nature and close to the earth. He tried the twenty-minute walk to the grocery store with reusable bags. This was a fun adventure but was not workable in his current circumstances, and it did not have the large impact that he so desired. The current structure of society and most communities do not accommodate this type of person.

The irony of The Well is that the road to a simpler life is very arduous and complicated; it is anything but simple. It takes years, and at times it feels impossible. We who have drunk from The Spring are now few and far between; we currently cannot find and connect to each other and are currently misplaced. The industrial revolution happened. Modern cities and infrastructures are designed around the automobile, not pedestrians, especially the community in South Ogden where his condo had been. Except for the beautiful trail by the river, it was virtually a concrete jungle and he was taking his life into his own hands anytime he wanted to go outside the city. With the current typical city design (or lack thereof), it is not natural to be the one bicycling to the health food store to get his exercise and time outside. Neither is it plausible while trying to stay vegan to buy organic sweet potatoes as a main staple. Calorie for calorie, it simply is not affordable.

Back in 2011, he saw these (his vegan diet and walking or bicycling as transportation) as steps forward, but still as only pieces, fragments. He needed more calories than he could afford to fuel his only form of transportation—bicycle and boots. Then he saw that ideally, he should plant his own food, ideally in his own yard— enough to sustain himself and his queen. This would be hard to do from a condo, but he decided to pitch the idea to the HOA. He knew that he could do some good, set an example and possibly even start a new local movement in the area. He was excited for his great idea to start a small community garden on the condominium complex instead of its endless lawns of Kentucky bluegrass (planted in a desert) and un-utilized grounds. He took the necessary preparation time, gathered his thoughts and decided what he wanted to say and how he wanted to say it. Granted, he is approaching a bunch of elderly people from the Great Depression and baby boomers, but surely, they would jump at the idea of someone volunteering to start a community garden for residents of the Sherwood condominium complex. The HOA denied his request almost instantly. It was not given a second thought.

Still, his discouragement is only minor because he has an epiphany: He and his queen would sell their condo and move to a location where they could grow a big garden for themselves. He could prove his validity despite all the resistance, and mostly to her that he is at last a man. After all, it is a man's cherished desire to use his manhood, his skill and strength to provide for his wife. This is what we're told since grade school and women dig it, right? He also realizes that it would be ideal in every way. Guys, at least many of them, do great on the farm. For some it is where they belong. They are happier and are free to become the men they are meant to be. But this objective takes years to achieve. It's like going so far forward that it ends up being one gigantic circle, nearly back in time.

A plant-based farm offers the ideal environment for many men to thrive. In this environ, men spend much time outside receiving exercise, sunshine and fresh air. They receive time with nature and their mother earth, and they develop their strength and their skills while learning to delay gratification, a quality that is disappearing from modern life. They learn patience and the ability to think far ahead into the long term. They also develop their knowledge and aptitudes with gardening, and of the natural world. Like physical exercise, it is one of those things that nearly seem too good to be true because there are myriads of benefits lumped into one! They also learn much about the mysterious world of plants. They learn compassion and discipline throughout the day while strengthening their muscles, and they are never far from their family and loved ones, where their children or dogs have wide open, safe places and fields in which to play outside. It's beautiful—closer to the way things are supposed to be. The unbridled perpetuation of suburban sprawl is a terrible global mistake.

Current Office Space for the Urban Human of the Future

It is difficult to be in, or to witness people in jobs where they're unhappy. They are excellent at what they do. They can do it all; their boss and the clients love them. They have excellent benefits and good pay. The only challenge is that they don't really like what they do! This is a big one. Their long hours in the office do little to nothing for them. Their walls are full of plaques and awards, but they're daily grinding, always at the beck and call of someone else; it is their job to do so, always taking care of sick people in a sick society. They sit, sedentary for eight or more hours a day, five days a week in an office, warehouse, kitchen or cubicle, deprived of natural light, fun interaction with others or the wonders of nature. For some, it's their second or even third job in attempt to "make ends meet".

Instead, as we each begin to awaken, we become strong. In doing this we also become more self-sufficient. As a sick society becomes a healthy one, with one individual at a time *choosing* health, strength and individual empowerment, it will eventually change global economies. How is the monoculture of GDP working for us? When enough people demand change, we will eventually change our current, worn out, outdated structure of society. We no longer need to beg, grovel, bend the truth, or frenzy ourselves into the few remaining loopholes, all which are based on fear. We will no longer need to bend or manipulate the truth, because we will become a society based on truths and not lies rooted in greed and fear of lack. Instead, living our dreams will provide the dream jobs—the real ones, and the real American dream, living in abundance, and balance with leisure time for friends, family and pets all in balance with our mother nature.

Public and environmental health plays a part here too. Looking at the many historical benchmarks in human progress, we have come a long way. Humanity has survived plagues of viruses and bacteria and has discovered ways of defending ourselves against them. Good hygiene, sanitation, herbs, essential oils and being generally healthy and robust is the first excellent defense against pathogens. These microorganisms are less of a problem than they were during the early 19th century.

Now we face plagues of social problems and there is much work to do. We can and we must do better. Continuing industrial and suburban sprawl relentlessly will only bring about more social problems. As Chief Seattle said: "What we do to the earth, we do to ourselves." We have improved in leaps and bounds, but with the rapid vanishing of earth's resources, there is a shrinking window of time to get it right. We must get it right. People are starting to get it right, slowly but surely; but there are major mountains to climb. The tentacles of greed throughout multinational corporations, governments and wealthy individuals have had too much sway for far too long. They have little accountability to the populace and no responsibility for their carbon footprint so, it is essential for massive amounts of people and key organizations and institutions to get on board. Currently, individuals are spoon fed and processed right through the collective system of half-truths controlled and manipulated by media and industry. Some are lies. Others are half-truths. Some are conveniently misplaced truths. Others are simple complacencies in the system. Some are honest mistakes, but all are a byproduct of the weakened and sick society that has become ours, where the current mode and structure of mainstream society is outdated. Yet the masses continue to spin on the hamster wheel, wondering what life is about unable to figure out why they're unsatisfied and unhappy. Humanity is becoming a weak species. We don't have to accept this. We can change and become strong.

Adopting a philosophy of self-reliance combined with having more than one source of income per individual offers hope. There are many sources of residual and supplemental income using whatever abilities one has through independent work such as internet work, affiliate marketing, free-lance "gigs", or odd jobs whatever your skill set. You can either make more money or you can spend less. Your job could now be the one you really dreamed of. Too often, the brick wall realization is made halfway through to retirement that the job you've been doing for fifteen years is a source of unhappiness. The job is not what you thought it would be, nor is it what you were told it would be, especially if you work three of them to make ends meet. This is because society is built on someone else's dreams. Dreams which became a monopoly, and were rooted in greed—greed which choked out every other dream in its path to become gigantic and compensate for some insatiable need to compete, get ahead and hoard: greed. Yet monopolies are not even a fair opponent. There is no competing with a monopoly. This is one reason why our dreams have been lost to "do what we have to and what we've been told."

For the first time in human history, living one's dream, the life of *true abundance* that is not at the expense of another is now possible. Our ancestors would have shouted for joy had they seen the opportunity that is now ours. How they lived provides us clues. They had sun, fire and stones. We have technology as a gift to be used wisely, sustainably in method and materials. They had mules, goats and packing animals, which provide clean energy; we have bio-fuel engines. Now is the only time throughout all human history where we can use the best of both worlds toward a balanced, sustainable, healthy and happy existence for all.

CHAPTER 5

After the Collapse, Rebuild Right: Individuals Make Up Society

"Just as it is not feasible for one to be in tip-top fitness condition all the time, neither is it feasible to be in perfect wellness condition all the time. As humanity progresses together in well-being then total wellness becomes more feasible." –Owen Staples

So how does one begin living the *real* dream? We all feel the pinch of too much to do while on a budget trying to keep up with only so many hours in a day. That feeling of trying to run under water, expending every ounce of energy, but in the end, you realize that you're just spinning your wheels.

How does one stay out of debt? How does one live without taking on a monstrosity of a mortgage for the next thirty years, slaving away one's life, gone from it every day to pay off your shelter? It takes time, and you may have to forego that 3-bedroom suite in the city or that brand new SUV in your garage—at least for now. However, with a sound plan, with the desired result in mind, you can accomplish your goal of living within your means and the true abundant life of freedom, not slavery. Fortunately, this can also equate to living lightly on the earth, in harmony with mother nature. It is a win-win situation!

Individuals can stop settling for whatever is offered, and instead engage in the practice of expecting quality that is the product of an honest and "right" (from the Buddhist meaning) livelihood. Don't settle for mediocrity. Expect quality, choose quality and insist on it, but also *be* it. This will take practice, so be patient and be good to yourself and remember that expecting quality does not mean becoming a snob. We have slowly been seduced by impersonal mass-produced goods with a low price tag, and we have forgotten the thrill of knowing the artisan who baked our bread or sewed our wallet, and the obvious feel of hand-crafted quality in our hands. We can be the artisan of something, while enjoying the quality goods provided by others striving for the same common goal: sustainable abundance and freedom.

Individuals who have more than one source of income enjoy a change in their routine and in case of a shortage in one source; they have others to fall back on. This also helps to change the economy to one that is service based. For example: a person has their regular job that gives back to the community and the earth by producing and selling sustainable goods, and services, instead of a greed-based retailer that coaxes people to buy more of what they don't need by using schemes of psychology in their advertising to manipulate people into making additional purchases or rack up credit card debt. An economy that is service-based and individual-centric is the key to freedom rather than our current capitalism/consumerism economy that is solely dependent on the ever increasing production and consumption of goods, consuming the natural resources of the earth and turning individuals into mindless drones. This approach is a dead end and only ensures that capitalist economies with their insatiable monopolies will eventually fall leaving very little behind with which to rebuild correctly.

In the south of France, shingles consist of clay tiles molded to the concave shape of a U. Each individual tile can simply be replaced when one is broken or damaged. This is in stark contrast to repairing a shingle roof here in the U.S.A., which easily runs into the price of $50,000. Additionally, garages are costly accessories of the average suburban home as well, their maintenance with many moving parts can run into a lot of wasted money. Owning and maintaining a home (shelter) has become so outrageously priced that with the current model it is no wonder most of our lives is spent at work. We spend 70+ hours per week sometimes between three jobs; and still for many, after bills are paid little money is left to be saved. Further, debt, including credit card debt is usually an inevitability to afford the basics. This is backwards and wrong. You are being duped. We are processed, controlled and conditioned right up and down the system. The puppet master wants it thus and currently has his way.

Aftermath

It is through the completion of this arduous journey that he truly understands poverty. A lot has happened to him in fifteen years. He has seen the same cycle of financial hardship and pain from many different angles. From deep in the abyss, to catching glimmers of hope, to hope in the form of $10 per hour jobs, which is not a livable wage. On this wage, a single person living alone can eat or pay rent. They cannot do both. It is the cycle that represents all different pieces but, in the end, only more spinning of wheels. The problem boils down to trying to have simply the basics—a house with picket fence, a wife, a dog, some pets, and a garden—all on ten dollars per hour. On this wage, the price of everything he wanted was just enough to buy them but not enough to retain them. Of course, they were. Prices are all determined by the puppet master. America is an oligarchy. Sure, there were times of bliss and times of reprieve, joy and even coasting ease. But it was always just enough to anesthetize him back into robot mode to continue the earning, buying and spending merry-go-round and the same thing continued as the spin cycle was stuck on repeat. This is a systemic problem. We are defined by Gross Domestic Product. It has become the measuring device for everything, and this no longer serves humanity.

He thinks of poverty as a person physically exerting himself to the max, running on empty in every way with the belief that with enough exertion, he will eventually escape the force of gravity and achieve lift off. But the fuel always runs out before lift-off is achieved, making the next attempt harder and less possible than the previous attempt. Who is he fooling? He can wish until doomsday. This will not wish fuel into his perpetually empty tank or grant him exemption from gravity. He is stuck. It is a continuous cycle of trying to squeeze and stretch mileage driven on a buck here and there of gas.

The horse must be placed in front of the cart for his success and for anyone's; it stands to reason. The model must be logical, rational, sensible. Currently it is not. Manipulation and monopolies are designed for the few at the expense of the many. For the pursuit of real happiness, this same rationality must be established and set up to serve every level—from individual to societal. That is, the idea of 'equal opportunity', which has been a lie.

As he wasted time and energy putting the pedal to the metal but only spinning his wheels he began to believe that the entire universe had turned against him. There is no doubt about it. He worked hard at those temp jobs for $10 per hour or less (with only the one exception of the printing press, which eventually was also cut to $10 per hour). Through it all he realizes that this is bigger than just him. Something in society is badly amiss. Something is cruelly unfair that causes a man to lose everything including his wife and home. An ever-increasing number of people are being told to work hard, keep going and it will eventually pay off, but they continue to scramble to make ends meet. The finish line keeps getting moved further away; it is to no avail and they remain in poverty always chasing that promise. It is a convenient oversimplification that we are not told about as we sign away our lives for that 30 year mortgage on our shelters.

Two memoirs were essential to tell the full story to wrap up the experience and the newfound ways that he will be referring to and teaching about. While the losses were incredibly painful and the path very rocky, abundance flowed in other ways to get him through the hardship, and after the hardship he knows a better way...

"When you lose, don't lose the lesson."
-The Dalai Lama

Functional Directionality

At the time of this writing, due to his single male low-income bracket status in 2017, he is finally able to receive federal grants to return to college and complete his college education. This helps him to realize that the system can work, if all the right circumstances line up at the right time, and for this he is beyond grateful. However, he still asserts that the system as a whole usually does not benefit people in his shoes, and the damage done and losses sustained in his life is irreparable and irretrievable. The system still *must* change. He hopes that awareness, exposure and disclosure will begin to change things in the right direction. Instead of evil, he believes the most fitting word for American government and current consumer capitalism is complacency. He concludes that the government (indeed all governments) need to be willing to spend the money necessary to "stand up and tell the truth to the people." (McDougall, 2016). They must introduce a new model, one that better serves the people in their "equal opportunity pursuit of happiness" by encouraging sustainability, human health and living harmoniously within the bounds of our mother earth.

He was grateful to acquire a part-time grocery job for the military base close to his parents' house in 2017. This meant that he didn't have to commute as far to work; it was a good job while he worked on his degree. In the fall of 2019, he completed his degree with excellent grades, graduating from Weber State University with a Bachelor of Science degree in Health Promotion and a minor in Zoology. He generally began to feel better about the world and realized there was, and still is, hope after all. Albeit, during his battle with the current collective disease rooted in a society desperately in need of reconstruction, he will never forget the lessons...greed, the widening inequality gap and disparities certainly exist. The perpetrators of this inequality like to remain undercover so that everything appears smooth on the surface, yet subtly they do their dirty work, permeate and encroach throughout society and throughout the world.

He has gone full circle. He is better and wiser for the major curve balls thrown at him throughout life; and the pain, the detour of 15 years where he gained everything—and then lost it—twice—was not without purpose. He learned the reason for this. It was not his fault. He worked very hard to keep all of it. In part this is what inspires him to write. The path found him, merely by his seeking to do what people do. That is his first lesson. Just as he was spinning his wheels, mainstream society is also merely spinning their wheels blindly, bulldozing into oblivion while the government further delays in dragging their heels as a few gigantic industries further lobby and manipulate to endlessly increase their profits and their domination of the world. This is indeed very concerning. He cannot recommend the current path of consumerism hand in hand with capitalism to anyone. He hopes that he has blazed a trail for others on his way out of the pain of his collapse and will leave behind some bread crumbs, some clues for people to consider as a guideline for life and eventually, for a new and improved foundation for society, toward building sound structures that work for every individual—a new hope for humanity.

He knows that this dream, this hope is big. He knows what he wants and doesn't want from life. This is now a blessed relief to have learned this earlier than later. He feels fortunate having learned it albeit through a rocky path. From his arduous journey, he feels more prepared for all his future decisions in life. Better jobs that pay a living wage, higher education, and the pursuit of romantic relationships are all now within the realm of possibility. For the first time in his entire life he has a real chance at these. He has his priorities straight and feels prepared for part two of his life which he awaits with joy and anticipation.

No matter how dark things get, there is always a light side. There is always hope. You always have options, and you are not a victim unless you accept that view. But you do need to act, make responsible choices, and take a stand. Speak up. Forget neutrality.

From this wild ride of 15 years he gains much. He has learned and grown on the journey and has become a better person, more refined and much stronger as a conscious citizen and consumer. He has gained wisdom, vision. He can see the extreme imbalance, the irony of current society. Regarding it and the future of humanity, he has hopes, but also doubts and grave concerns. There is no doubt that he still bears the scars of his own battles. He knows he cannot rescue humanity from themselves alone. Repairing the damage done by fear and greed to the earth, to tribes, communities, societies, economies and global relations will require many hands on deck— millions. It will require a revolution of millions of people demanding change toward compassion, rationale, unity, cooperation, sense and sustainability over greed, monoculture and domination.

There is too much at stake. We are dangerously divided. To disagree with another's value system, viewpoints or priorities is essentially an act of war. People are intensely passionate about what they believe and disbelieve. It is a daily cold war, which builds further resentments and causes more division, more exclusion. We have said indeed that these divisions are okay and that the lower price matters more than human health, relationships, and more than human connection. Meanwhile, the actions of giant industries speak ever louder that profits are more important than human rights;

this is the disease of greed. The political slogans that we fight over eventually fade but the division remains. Well, it is the world we live in and we have bought into the lies for far too long. It's time now to make some major changes. It is time to get going.

This year, 2020 is an election year. At the time of this writing, March 2020 there is much fearmongering, or perhaps the author's own coined term "fear-heroin" is a better term. The entire world is in turmoil and panic generated by the Corona virus (COVID-19). It is being blown way out of proportion by a monoculture media that sees only hype and dollar signs and who doesn't research the facts before rolling out a story. Many small businesses throughout the country are in financial ruin.

We are long overdue. It is time to fix the irony of this settling for disease, mediocrity, blindness, the cold war and the spiritual and energetic violence that is now the norm. Remember the words of Chief Seattle, "What we do to the earth, we do to ourselves." The warming of the earth's atmosphere is making the spread of tropical diseases much more likely. It is not too late to live in harmony with our mother earth. It is not too late to choose The Well, The Spring. We have choices, options and we have a voice. We do it because it matters. We can treat what matters like it *matters,* because we know it does. We have been there, done that and now we know what matters most. We now know better.

We must use our voice. We must act like our lives depend upon it, because they do. This matters and we need to start acting like it. We have the knowledge, benefit and hindsight of history, and we now know better. We must collectively be mindful and resist. We can take a stand against the giant-machine-caterpillar- puppet-master that threatens us all.

He knows it is time to separate the clutter from what is precious, wheat from the chaff the myths from the truth. It is important not only for him but for all beings. It is time to pull off the blinders and see the truth. At a time when people and the earth need clarity the very most, they are slyly manipulated, misled and ironically confused about health, wellness and environmental stewardship; people even doubt our connection to and reliance on the earth and all life.

The main perpetrators of this deception are a worn out "disease-care" system, greedy, politicians, giant industries and the media. For example, the paleo diet, another name for the Atkins or South Beach diet is a myth. It illustrates all starches as 'bad' with aggressive propaganda *confusing* the masses by 'bad' words such as 'carbs,' which now elicits a phobic response. The brainwashing has been that effective. While being a strict vegan may not be the answer for everyone, 'low carb' or any form of Atkins or paleo diets (high in animal products) are too far on the other side of the spectrum for humans. They are a poor choice for human health, the environment and for animals. "Good Almighty," what more is needed? Humanity is nearly out of time. There is not enough land, water and resources to sustain 8 billion (and increasing) people who are all trying to live more like Americans in adopting the Standard American Diet, (SAD) with increased meat and dairy, waging of war on the earth's resources. We cannot be fools and continue to expect our God of peace and love to make up the difference for our own complacency and denial. We have done just that for far too long, and we are already on borrowed time.

Amidst his journey he grew quite fond of two groups of people in America: women and Native Americans. He knows that with these two groups there exists tremendous power. Within these groups lie the catalysts for major positive change in America and across the entire world. However, the irony of these two groups is what he observed mid-way on his journey: Both groups are among the most underserved and manipulated, and therefore kept powerless by the system. If women were to realize that they have been blinded and misguided, and had their priorities turned upside down, distracted by materialistic desires that serve to anesthetize them with a temporary, sugar-like satiety, then the world would flip on its axis. The women of the world hold enormous power.

He hopes women come as their *authentic selves,* strong felines, awake and stripped of clutter to join the canine men at the gym, not in competition, but in cooperative, unity creating and training to resist the nonsense. Men are working to overcome their collective foolishness. He hopes that women will retire their princess syndrome and join us.

In a late-night flight of fancy, this poem came into being:

If men are canines then women are felines.
For a celebratory occasion they meet
where the drum beats at the tournament of sparring dogs;
The felines quietly watch, but loudly.
All present are accompanied by the beautiful
melody of the observing felines.
What are dogs without felines,
the yang without the yin?
The two combined in unity are divine.

He loves women's compassion that comes naturally for animals, children and their fellow canines and felines. He loves the spice they add to every recipe, the breeze they bring that stirs any stayed moment. Their capacity for patience, forgiveness, longsuffering and compassion gave him hope at a time when he felt it was all futile.

He has hopes. He would like to see the women of America reclaim their power, strength and vision, becoming self-sufficient and tune-in to their tribal nature, rooted deeply, strongly to the real nourishment of spirit, mind and body of their mother earth. He hopes they will tap into the source to soak in The Spring and drink from The Well to help spring forth the good life of true abundance. It is true abundance that for America is long overdue— the abundance of living in harmony with the land, compassionately, sustainably, responsibly. This real joy and true abundance is the true 'fun' that we all crave.

Native Americans are a deeply spiritual people, and are not yet fully numbed, diluted or anesthetized away from the lifeline to their earth and creator as are many European Americans. They have a wonderful lighthearted and witty sense of humor; they are survivors. These two traits are their greatest assets. Native Americans have retained their connection to Mother Earth, spirituality, healing arts. He would like to see them share their knowledge and understanding and spiritual knowledge, their abundant gifts in healing both people and planet. They are still very much in tune with these. Both women and Native Americans are currently comfortably numb, held just where they are wanted by the "disease-care" system, the meat and dairy industries, the media and certainly the puppet master. Owen pleads with these two groups to take care, heal yourselves so that you can grow in joy and help heal others and the planet, which is a step into true joy and true abundance, living your true dreams, which is the life that we were all intended to live.

CHAPTER 6

Here We are and Here We Must Change-Now

It is very concerning the way the system keeps people in compliance using what is basically soft force. Force is not the answer. He is all too familiar with it because it is so much like the HOA where "if you are in 'good standing' you can have your liberties…"

As mentioned, as recently as 2016 before returning to college, he believed that the U.S government was completely evil. He has since tempered that belief and now finds the word "evil" to be a bit harsh, at least if it is spoken in absolute terms. He believes two words that most fit are complacency and denial. Without a doubt, corrupt individuals within the government who have nefarious agendas do exist, and it would be a good thing for them to be fired and/or voted out. Much time is wasted by the time a bill passes through fifty offices "in processing." It is a sad day when the government, "big brother" and the media become the entity that nobody likes or trusts because they have sinister, secretive agendas of their own, where much is done to deliberately confuse and mislead the masses. Yet here we are in 2020 with just that to deal with. "We need a government that will stand up and tell the truth to the people." (–McDougall, 2016).[4] A government by consent of the governed is inherently an inspired idea that could work and has worked earlier in American history. With such a diverse and rapidly changing world, advanced technology and rapidly vanishing resources a sound governing body is necessary. But this is not the case. Currently, greed carries the day. If government is the machine, the operators of the machine have been gigantic corporations, extremely wealthy individuals and the largest industries.

This is not the time to try to sensor people's speech or dictate what they are "allowed" to say and talk about via social media and even who they interact with at social gatherings. Instead, and perhaps more than ever before it is a time to listen to people's concerns and introduce a new model that better serves people and the planet. It is time for people, *we the people* to speak up and out. Government can listen for a change.

Religions regularly condemn selfishness, but only the person-blame-approach is used. Nothing is mentioned about considering the system-blame, and the fact that many of our current problems stem from the worn-out structures of society and capitalism that created this selfishness, extreme individualism and other vices in the first place; individualism at the most extreme spectrum could loosely be called narcissism. Sins of immorality are condemned by many faiths, but no alternative is offered. Couples who live together, or "shack up" to save expenses are condemned, sharply labeled as sinners. They are then added to the repertoire of why the world is so evil and 'why it is going down', by a rich, white Christian who basically has money to burn and sees in black and white with tunnel vision. It is not considered that they are trying to make ends meet as individuals on $10 per hour employment, or worse yet, minimum wage.

Further, people become bored. They lack a sense of purpose. Society has made our purpose all the same: GDP and consumerism: earn, spend and buy, then repeat. Forever. Capitalism has been too aggressive, and religion has been too passive without really taking a stand on the damage that capitalism has done. We are being corralled like livestock right to where we are wanted, distracted, conveyed and anesthetized with fake sugar-like satiety. The result is that well-meaning religion is the left hand of capitalism. It spoon feeds trusting, innocent people right into the system of consumerism, played on repeat through the loud megaphone of media, where marriage, the only correct option as told by some, is now big business—one that is as competitive as a BYU vs. U of U football game.

Large corporations with swing shifts and open availability employ many people, and on one hand, they can allow for some disadvantaged people to get a fair start. It is the rules, regulations, policies and procedures of these big corporations that makes them safe for hiring someone with a disability; someone who may be on and off the street, or who may be struggling in life with addiction, poverty, homelessness, or mental illness as was just the case with the author—and he is forever grateful for that first job at the hardware store. Large corporations provide a starting point for these individuals—gives them a chance when no one else will even glance at their resume. On the other hand, the impersonal side of corporations requires open availability resulting in a topsy-turvy schedule, often for just under the number of hours that would require them to provide benefits to the employee. This is usually motivated by greed of the stock market and expectations that the corporation's stock will continually increase in value. It is a vicious cycle of greed combined with economic monopoly and a desire for limitless increase with no regard for the social, economic, or environmental consequences; it seems as though giant multinational corporations really do want to own the earth. Corporations attempt to squeeze as much work as possible from low-wage employees, cramming these into stressful swing shifts and odd hours. Employees are therefore stressed, overworked and underpaid. This leads to chronic stress, work related injury and poor health. It allows for a low quality of life to become the norm and the accepted standard. From a health promotion standpoint this is ridiculous! It is treating people like robots and numbers where all that matters, all that *can* matter, is shopping where the price is the lowest.

It is an interesting side note that at the time of this writing all the land (estimated 6 acres) around the integral part of this story, the Episcopal church, is currently for sale. It will undoubtedly be turned into more "disease-care" buildings, pushing big pharma and medical clinics. When this happens so close to the church, the land will be ruined; it will only be a matter of time until that historic church is torn down to become a fleeting building to house the next up and coming cellular phone rave. Then the cycle will continue; the business that occupies the new building will change every few years.

This memoir is a typical representation of an average American's life. We have been using the same mode and model since the industrial age, and it is badly outdated. This is the wakeup call for all of us that we are not meant to do this anymore. We never were. We have gone too far. Living the life of consumption is not living; we are slowly killing ourselves. It is slow, steady suffocation. The earth may or may not survive, but if we continue with that mindset, we place extreme difficulties on ourselves as collective humanity, one where we very well could reach the point of inflicting irreparable damage and face human extinction. The current way without modification and improvements is a dead end, literally. It is death; humanity is in danger and could soon be facing extinction.

Other countries are foolish to try to adopt the exact current American model of capitalism. A new model of capitalism,(if we insist on calling it that) is necessary. It is imperative to reach a point of balance between profit and planet. How many hundreds, thousands of locations across the globe does one company need? Individually, corporations can reach a point where they have satisfied their need for growth and they can virtually say: "I have enough." This is an empowering stance for individuals, and it would also be empowering for corporations. Since greed is a disease and often will not reach this point, governments must be in a position to regulate the greed until it can be healed. It is inhumane and flat out wrong that the few in the name of greed are allowed to take down everything and everyone, (the few at the expense of the many). But currently our government works not as regulators of, but *as business partners to* these huge corporations. They need to be reinstated to their original role as regulators. (Popper, 2019). [5]

In subscribing to a specific faith, hyper-religiosity and blind obedience, both of which can be signs of collective mental illness, is not the answer. Where some have already learned this, others have yet to see it. The author learned this the hard way.

Marriage as an institution originated and continues with good intentions and can serve as a security net that can help to curb selfishness. It can also stand as a safer route than promiscuity and as a sexual outlet for one of the strongest drives in the human body. But it may not be the only way for everyone; and if it is the only way, as many faiths assert, there must be a practical setup, such as a community, and ample allotted time for others to learn until they can fully understand and accept this, not shoved down their throat, or as though they must race for it, or that they are too unintelligent to understand—this is elitism. Neither should it be taught in all or nothing, black and white terms and that everyone should just grow up and get married as soon as possible because it's "just what you do," and if you don't, you're damned.

The world has changed from the days when deity began talking to a desert tribe more than 4,000 years ago. It is commendable and self-sacrificing for two people to make a commitment to each other, in any family structure, and it requires hard work to keep that commitment faithfully and the love healthy and strong. However, it should not be taught that marriage is the only way for salvation, success, happiness and to do right in the eyes of God. Instead, freedom to choose on multiple levels must be both granted and encouraged. Our world is too diverse to swallow, believe, practice and accept marriage as the destination all at once. The new setup must consider factors such as individual's style and pace of learning and their current socio-economic status. It must be accepted that a person can engage in freedom to choose all the way through their learning. If marriage must adhere to a specific code, to be only a certain way as proposed by many religions, then these very religions need to have a sound program that helps people to accomplish it and live comfortably, within that religious community, for example.

This means that this system would ensure that financial needs, moral guidance, sexual orientation are all covered, and there must be an achievable route to accomplish the proposed standard of marriage. It should not be out of reach financially for anyone regardless of income. Some people fall through these loopholes based on the few details that an ancient record of a desert tribe gave about it 4,000-2,000 years ago. Marriage is not the be-all-end-all for everyone; neither is having children. The pressure to marry that is placed on young individuals, whether directly or indirectly, is an added pressure in an already stressful day and age. This pressure causes a lot of problems, financial struggles, unplanned children and ironically, broken families. It is wrong to withhold contraception from anyone for religious or societal reasons. Freedom to choose combined with sound education to make a *choice* must be respected and reinstated.

Religion mentions a sick, sinful and troubled world and that the proposed sect is a sanctuary from it. Yet, one must go out into that sick world to earn a paycheck. It is this "filthy lucre" that pays tithes, alms and offerings. In days of old, sects, mosques, synagogues, and monasteries were as autonomous and self-sufficient as possible without required tithes; some of these were entirely self-sufficient. [6] In fact, these helped the destitute and needy from that self-sufficiency.

The current model is a trap, (whether intended or not) with leaders misusing authority on human sexuality. Rigid religions create an automatic bind. One option is to give in to the second strongest drive in the body—human sexuality next to hunger and thirst for water, and live "in sin." Christianity shames sexuality. It is a self-defeating form of social Darwinism and creates more exclusion, self-righteousness and elitism—the exact opposite of the very core of Jesus' teachings—the love and inclusion of everyone. Further, and ironically these do damage to religion itself. It causes negative associations, where people see at the forefront the over zeal and disparities that religion creates and causes them to miss the good core that exists therein. Their other option is to get married at a very young age so that they can be free with their sexuality within the sanctity of marriage "the right way" the decision is usually heavily influenced by fear and the avoidance of guilt; but then the couple faces the reality of money arguments, financial stress, possible unplanned children and a very real possibility of divorce in only a few years. They were not prepared for these in any way lacking the maturity at such a young age; they were certainly not sufficiently mature emotionally and far too often completely unprepared financially and their understanding of money.

The current setup is not realistic. Perhaps 2,000 years ago it was, but modern expectations on individuals are a bipolar and unrealistic cultural norm, the way faiths put a blanket statement with blanket rules over the masses with no account, no room for individual personality, means, abilities or circumstances within the extreme individualistic western society that America has become. Religious guidelines are just that—guidelines. They do not apply to every person the exact same way since they can't consider circumstances or timetables.

Everyone is now allowed their own individual timetable to learn, practice, apply and accept. This is because each person is different and has their own personality, likes and dislikes. To spoon feed people and treat them as though all people are the same just like sheep is too much like herding sheep. There are now other creatures that share the pasture with the sheep. There must be the understanding that as individuals awaken and become new creatures, there will be differing viewpoints. These individuals are evolved; sheep have evolved. Collective humanity has a clearer understanding of the overall nature of things now, too much to be treated as lemmings. We can grow and develop at an individual pace, acknowledging that we are individuals with a voice and that there is room to accommodate reasonable wants and needs. This must be accounted for in individualistic societies, (Canada, Western Europe, United States). The habit of applying blanket statements and rules attempting to control the masses is a worn-out habit born of fear; it is medieval. There may be sheep who need careful upbringing, and it is wise to give them the nurturing they need while they grow. But evolve they can and evolve they do. They each have a purpose, and the various creatures can all coexist together.

People in certain cultures virtually grow up inside the cathedral and then must make sense of the outside world full of their opinions from the standpoint of everything they learned while deep inside the archives of the cathedral. They are unprepared for the world outside, having been sheltered throughout their entire upbringing, yet they attempt to apply the cathedral archives to the outside world and to every situation for answers. Canned answers are applied the same to every question under the sun. Even everything they think they know and understand about the earth begins from somewhere within the cathedral archives or vault and it is all supposed to fit within the very narrow confines of everything they already "know." It is a battle between inductive and deductive reasoning.

The creationist viewpoint of the earth's age being no more than 10,000 years does not instantly have to conflict with the evolutionary standpoint of the earth being 4.6 billion years of age. People are kept from the truth, manipulated through media, politics and religion. Evolution is fact. Mathematical formulas of carbon and radioactive dating and decay can be applied to determine the age of the earth and the moon with accuracy. Deliberate ignorance and denial create flawed thinking and misconstrued beginning viewpoints for a journey through *life*. And, ironically, it leads to the loss, confusion and further spiritual blindness, (about which Jesus himself lectured strongly) of large amounts of people. It causes big misinterpretations. Some of the most profound events in religious history took place in nature, rather than a man-made building. The sacred grove, the burning bush, Jesus fasting in a desert or from a high mountain, which The New Testament outlines clearly that he visited often. Jesus frequently visited mountains; he was crucified on a tree, Yggdrasil and Odin hanging from the world Ash tree as he suffered, the Buddha sitting beneath a Bodhi tree for several days… These are the experiences that move people and things where traditions of passion and fixed belief are formed.

However, there is still so much emphasis placed on being inside the workings of the cathedral for many hours, deep into the archives and the ancient records and further, making this out to be life and all that is, instead of seeing clearly that this is man's interpretation and a system built upon it. Life is life; there is no life but life. It is the grass, insects, animals, trees and sunlight which form our earth and all life, all provided by the sun and the creator. We people also fit into this creation (life as life) in a unique light as our own kind of creatures. We are not separate from life or from the earth and universe, however, current society, and certain aspects of religion teach otherwise. There is the cathedral, (or synagogue, or mosque), the grounds just beyond the cathedral, synagogue or mosque, cultivated and domesticated. Then, there is the living and wild forest that surrounds these man-made buildings. These three portions of landscape are all very different; they are not the same. Yet, each has its rightful place and its part of the plan. This must be understood and accepted.

1. The cathedral interior (mosque, or synagogue)
2. The cathedral grounds
3. The living forest teeming with life that surrounds the cathedral.

The next time you feel overwhelmed and are unable to see the forest for the cathedral walls, you can remind yourself of these three distinct areas. They each have a place, but it should be understood that they are each different for a reason and that each is needed with a place in the modern day, and that there is organization and unity desperately needed on a global scale that accommodates each of these differences. You may also find it helpful to take a break from the cathedral and spend some time outside in nature for a season. Well-informed, receptive, flexible and educated people make a more solid foundation.

Ancient records of people's dealings with God are a timeless gift. We are glad to have these. However, these are not a perfectly intact historical record, and we should not interpret every verse literally when it was written thousands of years ago and was copied and translated an unknown number of times. The world has changed drastically since then, and this change was brought about mostly by humans.

It is also unfair of faiths to discourage people from finding their own individual path as part of finding and knowing oneself. To prevent individual growth is fear-based. It is a form of controlling the masses. There must be balance here. It is generally seen and taught that individuality is selfish and the pursuit of one's own desires, interests and passions is wrong, "sinful." Yet "knowing thyself" is essential to understanding ones' likes, dislikes, personality and is ultimately a principle of spiritual growth. Only capitalism can create this opportunity for individual growth, but only the current model of capitalism can twist it wrongly into the extreme to the detriment. Excess ego boosting and growth at the expense of all else with nobody and nothing else considered at some point becomes destructive in its selfishness to one's authentic self and outward with the ripple effect poison leeching into society. After all, what would happen if all 8 billion of us tried to do just that all at the same time with nobody and nothing else considered? The answer of course is chaos.

One path can and does enhance another, advances, diversifies and enriches the learning. It is restrictive and confining to insist on only one pasture to sheep who don't yet know better. "Men shall not live by bread alone." –Jesus of Nazareth, King James Version of the Bible.

Current knowledge can be enhanced by the path of self-exploration, and that path also enhances their faith. Seeing things slightly differently (from Islam to Judaism, to Buddhism, to Christianity for example) offers a refreshing perspective. Seeing where there is some overlap can be faith promoting not faith destroying. Due to the many implications that we are all basically to *do* and to *be* the same thing while having no account for people's individual needs or challenges and no set up for various life stages of growth maturity especially in the spiritual sense, is flawed. Jesus was about the purpose and spirit of the law more than the finite hiccups and hang-ups, or to callings extended by a bishop or other official in the name of, and in absolute adherence to the letter. In fact, he regularly condemned just that in tense moments with Sadducees, Pharisees and publicans rebuking them as "hypocrites!" –New Testament, King James version of the Bible.

The universe, or God, can speak to people *as* and through individuals. "Building the kingdom which is nigh at hand" will require many gifts, abilities, talents, experiences and individual personality types as instruments. This also encompasses all faiths. Yes, all faiths. It is all-denominational. It is not a Hindu, pagan, Muslim, Jewish, or Christian department. It is *universal* unity. Each has a place. The spiritual and energetic warfare needs to stop. There should be no inadvertent disrespecting of one another over whose truth is more true or powerful. All faiths have some truth. There should be an open-door policy where all are welcome to come and taste of the fruits. Let others choose and taste of the delicious fruits of truth for themselves according to what they need at the time on their journey. Let them do the choosing for themselves as freedom to choose is in every way once again reinstated.

As far as his being born and raised in the LDS (Mormon) church he has had mixed feelings, but he managed to reach his own conclusions. He knows some good people in the LDS faith. He appreciates the safe and family-like atmosphere, the friendliness, the sense of community and people that will basically drop whatever they're doing when they are called upon to help another. This is a rare gem in this day, and he appreciates that people like this still exist. However, he also sees needed change in other areas. He experienced a lot of unnecessary suffering, and he knows that others do as well. His limbs were caught between the gears of Mormonism and capitalism and he was trapped, stuck for 40 years. The promises of the latter as blessed by the former caused him to find a greater dream; what is currently called the American dream is hopeless and false. It appeases only a few at the expense of the many. He knows that Mormonism is still very much entangled in the gears of current societies and capitalism where everything still depends on GDP, and it certainly doesn't currently offer an alternative except to participate in the system of capitalism.

He knows there is more. He enjoys exploring it. He is at peace with the universe.

He believes that there are some good things taught in his LDS church, as with all faiths— and the church itself is the entity most in need of accepting this—there are other perspectives to consider. He sees that the LDS faith is generally a safe, wholesome and sound place for families and growing kids, and it's great that there is a haven available. However, it needs to be more live and let live. It is no longer necessary for all people to "multiply and replenish." Not everyone wants or should be coerced or pressured in any way to having children. This should mean that multiple forms of contraception and sex education should be widely available. This is one major area where free will must be restored; to have children or not should be a conscious, free choice, especially for someone who already lives in poverty, or is disabled, or struggles with addiction. He has evolved beyond the tunnel vision, and while he respects a wholesome model for raising a family, he doesn't feel the need to hang out much with those who live with tunnel vision. Just as returned missionaries don't typically hang out with the children from nursery; likewise, awakened ones don't typically grind elbows with those insisting on deliberate ignorance and tunnel vision from the hospital, nursery and bread factory of the cathedral folk.

He believes that it would be well for people to go straight to the source for answers in their prayers, as did the Mormon church's founder –Joseph Smith, who was a proponent of utopian societies and understood the essential principle of freedom to choose. When asked "how do you govern such a vast people as this?" Smith replied, "it is very easy, for I teach them correct principles and they govern themselves." (Bushman, 2005).[7]

It was not until many years later in 2015 during a visit to Europe while exploring the cathedrals of medieval Christianity that he reflects upon the significance of his experience with his Catholic girlfriend in 2001 inside the Episcopal church. In Europe the cathedrals were built centuries ago by hand, made largely of stone, taking decades sometimes even centuries to complete. He noticed the beauty of the stained-glass windows, outstanding architecture, live plants and the quiet, reverent atmosphere inside that invites reflection any time of day by people from all walks of life. He couldn't help but compare this to his being born into the Mormon faith where on a weekday one would have to make an appointment with the bishop just to get inside the church. There are no live plants, and the setup doesn't really allow for one to just walk inside the church throughout the week and meditate, pray, contemplate in reverence and beauty bathed in light as do the cathedrals of Europe. While that which is referred to as *modern revelations* by modern prophets of the LDS faith may not be without inspiration, he now clearly sees that they are inevitably entangled and filtered by many of man's agendas, fears, priorities and biases. LDS society is still very much entangled in the web of mainstream American capitalism.

In the LDS faith there is much emphasis placed on baptism by emersion being essential to salvation. The only option currently allowed is inside the church. Being baptized in the living waters of mother earth for example, amongst creation is not allowed. He believes there is a general fear and misunderstanding of anything that exudes natural or "earthy" in the faith because it resembles the "peace and love" of the 1960's, which, by default most believe automatically equates to sex, drugs and rock and roll. This is generally dreaded; it is fear-based thinking stemming from a faith that is afraid of and disconcerted by anything sexual in nature. Earthy somehow automatically equates to fear of nakedness and sex. Sex is a heavy, uncomfortable and shamed topic in the faith. The very word is practically taboo. However, it is a topic that comes up naturally, so natural discussion should be encouraged along with the study of sound educational avenues, the personal study of which should be expected and encouraged like any other fact of life. The author encourages enrollment in a Human Sexuality class taught at major universities. He hopes to see the day that the class is offered through the community at no charge. Those with lower socioeconomic status are especially in need of learning, understanding and personal study about the details of bringing other humans into the world. They too, as well as all people have the right to an informed choice in this regard.

With this misunderstanding of mother earth and her nature comes a tendency toward habitual avoidance and monoculture. To him it seems that the leaders are uninterested in doing anything different or new. There is an unwillingness to change anything, to branch out and accept new ideas, try new approaches, and consider alternative perspectives. Yet doing so is beneficial to mental health—individually to collectively; but this is not the case. They seem only interested in the perpetual continuation of tradition and what has always been done. This tendency toward what the author calls spiritual dementia takes place in the leaders of major faiths throughout the world. Jesus warned about spiritual blindness, wrongs in rigidity and unhealthy adherence to the letter of religious word. The author doesn't say this in vindictiveness but as an honest observation having seen, experienced, and suffered from it firsthand. He knows that diversity is the answer and variety does lighten any perpetually stagnant situation like a fresh breeze. He hopes there will be a place in teaching of the creator of all creation, the essential role of our mother earth, her bounty offered if we provide respect and reverence. Owen encourages the networking and installation of regular educational programs (besides Boy Scouts) and curriculums about sustainability, nature and where humans fit into creation from a respectful and hands on standpoint, and that evolution and creation need not be mutually exclusive, but instead can be mutually enriching in terms of learning. This is a vital beginning standpoint. Provide some clues and let others form their own conclusions about this as they begin the process of lifelong enjoyable learning.

As a promoter of healthy earth and lifestyles through plant-based diets and being well acquainted with the LDS Word of Wisdom found in section 89 of the Doctrine and Covenants, he often finds himself shaking his head. He recalls a conversation with his longtime reptile friend, who at the time held a leadership position in the bishopric. Owen was invited by this friend to a ward Christmas breakfast, but was unable to attend. A few days after the breakfast, the friend's words shed light on a glaring discrepancy and one item of LDS operations that continually leaves Owen baffled: "Hey man, I'm actually glad you couldn't come to that breakfast, you would have been pissed. Fifty pounds of bacon is pretty much a given at those things." Instances like these are what make him shake his head. Science has already confirmed the dangers to one's health of smoking and alcohol as plainly warned in the Word of Wisdom nearly two-hundred years ago. Now science is beginning to also confirm the dangers to human health and the planet from excess meat consumption. The Word of Wisdom also plainly reads: "they (beasts) are to be used sparingly; and it is pleasing unto me that they should not be used, only in times of winter, or of cold, or famine." (Doctrine and Covenants, 1833). Yet at these activities, "fifty pounds of bacon is pretty much a given." He wonders how this is hardly given a second thought and from leaders to members in these times, how it continues like business as usual.

The one size fits all approach for so many issues seems to him like something akin to corporate marriage promotion. It is curious that in a global church the majority of leaders shown are older, rich, white, married men. He hopes they embrace diversity in more ways than has previously been demonstrated, branch out some and try some different things.

CONCLUSION

As we as individuals begin to awaken, one by one, we bring the light, as well as meet it halfway. We bring our light to the collective light. It is already on its way. We realize that outside of the warehouses and the cathedrals dark enough to keep people inside of them where it is safe, there is a living forest, harmonious and abundant outside in the sun, the source of all real light and life. We can finally see this only real source of light. We are blessed by its radiance, its life-giving force, and its warmth. We will learn to cooperate, combine, turn the warehouses and cathedrals into our all-denominational cultural and recreation centers—still there, still available, still used, but differently from how they are now...

We can once again commune with our angels and walk with our Gods in a daily exchange as humans did in the ancient record of 4,000 years ago, but this is not so readily recalled. No one knows when the son of God cometh except God. The author believes that it is not a set date and he believes the modern problem of the rapid consumption of earth's resources changes the idea that it is a fixed date. Instead, it is contingent upon how things go and how we utilize the remainder of our period of probation while here. Striving to become wiser stewards, kinder, more compassionate citizens to all fellow beings will buy humanity time. Rather than come in destruction and devastation, it is possible for him to come in peace if we make the choice and align ourselves with life and stop squandering the days of our probation on what is now the unwise, inefficient use of earth's resources.

These gears of society that have become "the way it is" are making us weaker, not stronger. Debt, including a mortgage, makes one weaker. Poor health makes one weak. A job loss or resignation to search for something else should not make or break a marriage. Money as subordinate servant should be an attainable goal and not the master, especially for religious people as it is part of their beliefs. But the truth is that the overuse of the current model puts most Americans in a position where they are basically owned by their job, debts and money; they work to earn a paycheck but they have nothing saved; no surplus to cushion a hardship. It is all swallowed up by the overhead canopy of bills and debts. Financial stress and bondage make one weak. Relationships that become unhealthy through guilt, obligation and fear makes one weak. These are all part of the disease of the devolved masses. With any of these symptoms, one is at the mercy of government entities, HOA's, collection agencies, credit card companies, and unless one can keep up or pay up, there is no reconciliation and no mercy. An individual is owned and is just a dust particle in the giant machine, the vacuum. A person can earn more money, or simply learn to spend less.

It is now becoming more common for people to set aside society's norms and to live a life that is reasonable, environmentally responsible and downsized. The tiny home movement is one example of this. Currently, people trade their lives of thirty years working a 9-5 job to pay for their 30-year mortgage on their shelter. With tiny homes, however, a shelter is affordable. One can often pay cash. What is more, one often has the freedom to work part-time, and sometimes solely from home while living in a tiny home. It is closer to ideal for an increasing number of people.

The Trial

It's all on trial—his whole journey, but mostly it is he who is on trial. He was a fool. It's true that during his marriages, he thought mostly of himself. He was immature. He did his best with what he knew and what he had to work with. His critics were harsh. They judged him as they would an enemy. He had a lot on his plate, the odds stacked highly against him. Much happened; a lot of ground was covered, and through the pain he gained wisdom. He learned from the mistakes. It was one wild journey. He did his best with where he was at the time. He asks that the jury find him innocent.

The End

GALLERY

The author makes some recommendations to individuals seeking to avoid the traps described in his memoir:

1. **Eat less meat, especially cheap beef products, which damage the environment including the great rainforests. You don't need to become a strict vegan to be environmentally conscious and light on the earth. Aim for a plant-based diet. This means no more than 2-3 servings of meat per week. This will help to correct the major cause of environmental destruction of the entire planet: factory farming. This improves the health outcomes for both people and planet.**

2. **Less is More. Consider a "tiny home." This will set yourself free from thirty-years of slavery to a mortgage and a perpetual cycle of sickness and stress for our basic need—shelter. This cycle is nothing more than a band-aid and does not reach the underlying issue. Many individuals make up collective society and collective society has major problems, several big holes in the ship. It's time to repair them quickly. You have options and you have a voice. Enough demand brings results.**

3. **Get involved politically. 2020 is an election year. Vote (including locally). Your vote does count. People generally don't care until society's encroaching gears of greed begin to personally affect them. Eventually and surely, they will affect everyone. The time to act is now. Donate. Volunteer. Question authority. Become a conscious consumer and citizen. Ask questions, and insist on a rational, logical answer. More parties are needed as a valid choice on the ballots. Consider adopting the green party as the political party that will make true change-the change needed. Great things happen when we take care of our mother earth and make**

her a priority. This should be the standard. This is more than all-denominational. It is now universal.

4. Buy the eco choice as much as you can. This includes *local*, sustainable, fair trade and support of small businesses. Clothing, food, jewelry, cosmetics, art, organic food and décor are all excellent items for this. Refuse to take part in the fear, greed, corruption and monopoly by refusing to support gigantic multinational corporations that are not doing their part to help the environment, or who don't really take care of their employees.

5. Decide what you can do as a conscious citizen and to give back. See this as a journey as you awaken in joy, not a destination. Less is More. Reduce, Reuse, Recycle, Rethink. What can you do with these slogans as your goal? You will find that there is a lot and that you will begin to feel great about your choices and your new life.

6. Take Dave Ramsey's Financial Peace University and follow the steps, including cutting your credit cards. Get out of debt. Stay out of debt.

7. Don't buy tropical hardwoods or exotic animal skins. Refuse to support exploitation and species extinction.

8. Taste of the good fruits of all faiths, not bread only. Acquire your own soul food. Pay close attention to what resonates with you; explore that and similar paths in joy. Diversity is the answer. Accepting this is helping to manifest it.

"The more you know, the less you need." –Cody Lundin

APPENDIX

Suggested Reading and Study

**Food Over Medicine by Dr. Pam Popper and Glen Merzer.
Informed Healthcare:**
www.Wellnessforumhealth.com

**Owen's websites: Read the books; help to share the message, and
participate in the Ecomarkets:**

http://wellnessdiaries.com/
http://timelessecomarket.com/

Local Authors (Utah)

Memoirs of A Fallen Angel by Deeton Charles
Through Some Miracle Not Yet Clear to Me: The Nightmare of Living Under
the Dictatorship of Idi Amin and Surviving, by Vincent Musaalo
Catch Me If You Can... Scripted by Thought Continuum
Faery Sight by Patricia Bossano
Discovering the Word of Wisdom, Surprising Insights from a Wholefood,
plant-based Perspective by Jane Birch
www.Discoveringthewordofwisdom.com
Three Reluctant Promises by Kierstin Marquet

Health, Wellness and the truth about Current Society

Diet For A New America by John Robbins

Healing Environments by Carol Venolia
Well-Being the 5 Essential Elements by Tom Rath and Jim Harter
The Good-Life by Helen Nearing
The Gifts of Imperfection: Let Go of Who You Think You're Supposed to be and Embrace Who You Are by Brene Brown
Green Prosperity: Quit your job, live your dreams by Thomas J. Elpel

The New Good Life by John Robbins
The Truth About The Drug Companies by Marcia Angell, M.D.
Buddha and The Borderline by Kiera Van Gelder
Deadly Medicines and Organized Crime by Peter C Gotzsche
The Growth Delusion by David Pilling
Marriage, A History: From Obedience to Intimacy, Or How Love Conquered Marriage by Stephanie Coontz
A History of Marriage by Elizabeth Abbott

The author encourages study and education. Sound education is a key part of making a difference in societal change, which is a step toward allowing the individual life we want of living our dreams. While enjoying your learning at university and on your own, he especially recommends the following two classes as missing links to the complicated puzzle of our world:

Human Sexuality
Social Problems

www.Tinyhomes.com

Animals, Religion and Christianity:

God's Covenant with Animals by J. R. Hyland
Animal Theology by Andrew Linzey
Finding Darwin's God by Ken Miller
God Hates: Westboro Baptist Church, American Nationalism and the Religious Right
by sociologist, Rebecca Barret Fox. www. Anygoodthing.com
The Koran
Rough Stone Rolling by Richard Lyman Bushman
Saint Francis of Assisi by G.K. Chesterton

Outliers by Malcolm Gladwell
Snowflower and the Secret Fan by Lisa See
Who Gave Pinta to the Santa Maria by Robert S. Desowitz
The Celestine Prophecy by James Redfield

ENDNOTES

1   Our Sexuality
2   2013 Healthy Lifestyles Expo; "Get Healthy Now!"
3   Escape Fire documentary
4   You Tube: Why Doctors Don't Recommend Veganism #3, Dr John McDougall.
5   Dr. Pam Popper You Tube Video
6   Plantagenet Chronicles
7   Joseph Smith Rough Stone Rolling, Richard Lyman Bushman, 2005.